1

Praise for "The Nonconformist Salesperson" and Expertise of Dr Subayal Khan

Christian Moser: *The Founder of the One Life, One List system for simplifying your life and your business.*

Website: *http://thechristianmoser.com/*

Throughout my career I have closed sales with many renowned multinationals which has created great impact on society and helped in industry disruption. During this time, I have observed that the traditional sales techniques simply do not work. With an engineering background, I approached the sales from a problem centric perspective. This has allowed me to close sales with a much higher rate than my friends who had a concrete sales career as salespersons.

How your philosophy matches that of Subayal:

I have always been curious as to why my sales methodology is so effective and works each time. I have used it in software engineering business, in the project management business and also in other domains of business where I was active during my career. I met Dr Subayal Khan and discussed with him on a cup of coffee in London and at that time he was working on his book "Closing with conviction and confidence". We discussed about this dilemma and we had a lot in common. We both had an engineering background and we both were successful businessmen. Our sales methodology and approach were almost identical. Therefore, it was no brainer for Dr Subayal and me to collaborate. We immediately decided to bring that work to the German market in their native language.

Why in German Language:

At this point, he also told me about his love for German people and his one year that he spent in Erlangen in Fraunhofer IIS. He told me that he will like to involve me in taking the book to the German people. Also, since our philosophy of sales was so identical, we decided to edit, translate and adapt the manuscript to the German language. It was an important decision which we took. Afterwards, I have been working diligently and as his manuscript took the final form in English, so was the German version of it. In this way, we both decided to take this amazing work to the German market in German language so that the people there can read and enjoy it in their mother tongue. I firmly believe that collaboration and co-creation is the way to success and this book is a true reflects it.

Corbin Links: *CEO, Links Business Group LLC.*

"Mr. Corbin Links helps clients such as Microsoft, Cisco, Disney, The United States Government, Southern California Edison secure, scale, and automate their businesses, reduce costs, and run large IT programs".

Website: *https://corbinlinks.com/*

Due to Subayal Khan's consulting, and business strategic background we were able to take our course from just a few collective modules and build it into something that can scale of a massive size to any number of markets verticals and niches that our company is targeting. He literally sat down with us, walked us through a step-by-step process and added a lot of new ideas we weren't thinking of and with that I'm confident to say we're likely to get at least another six plus figures per year into that stream alone based on the course updates and material updates that we are working through with Subayal Khan's consulting expertise.

Another aspect I want to talk about just really quick is his expertise in sales in closing so we've worked with a lot of closers in our business I do a lot of closing our sales team does a lot of closing certainly we've done many years in the B2B space but I have seen few people that have his ability to quickly decide and discern what's going on what is the meat of the conversation what are the pain points what is really going on right because whenever we're in sales there's always a story behind the story and he's able to get to the heart of that quickly and then move to the next level of helping people understand what that big picture is what is the next result what's the transformation and he's able to do this with very large high ticket items in fact he's closed and built many programs with the EU and Finland and other areas that have been in the six seven eight plus figure range based on his abilities to not only close but build and manage teams effectively. Due to his strategic knowledge of business across many verticals he has the unique capacity and skill set to really be able to tune in and home in on what the best possible strategy and solution might be for any given situation. So, we cannot say enough good things about Subayal and if you're a serious business and you're selling high ticket items of let's say four figures and high four figures or you are looking for the strategy side of business to really understand where you are, where your clients are, what market dynamics are going on at any particular time? and want to adjust quickly and effectively to those with Subayal's suggestions and ideas, then I highly recommend that you give him a call or look him up through his websites: www.subayal.net. I cannot recommend him enough.

Usman Qureshi: *Chief Executive Officer at Vaulsys FZE.*

Vaulsys provides innovative payment options on all physical and digital payment touch points through an open platform. We also provide AML and FMS (Fraud Management Solution) for the banking, payments and financial industries.

Website: *http://vaulsys.net/*

The Nonconformist salesperson is one of the best reads regarding the challenging world of sales and business development. The book talks about the innovations in sales and how the traditional and outdated methods of sales are no longer effective. The book talks about addressing the needs and, also fulfil the cravings of a buyer. The book covers all the aspects of a sales process and presents a unique and innovative formula to go from start to finish by addressing the GAP between the current and the desired state. This book will challenge you to re-define your 'why' and transform you from being an average salesperson to a champion closer.

THE NONCONFORMIST SALESPERSON

"Unleash the nuclear power of unconventional wisdom, and mindset to become an authority in the area of sales"

–Christian Moser, http://thechristianmoser.com/

"This book by Subayal Uncovers: How an ultimate sale closer is forged from the elements of mindset, identity and trust? The unconventional wisdom in this book explores and diagnoses the way you can unleash the power of mindset, beliefs, strategies and techniques to achieve incredible success as a closer."

–Christian Moser, http://thechristianmoser.com/

Written by: DR SUBAYAL KHAN.

www.subayal.net

Adapted and Narrated in German Language by: CHRISTIAN MOSER.

http://thechristianmoser.com/

Author's name: Dr. Subayal Aftab Khan
Title of the book: The Nonconformist Salesperson.

To my wife and son

To Finland and its people for giving me the opportunity to excel in all areas of my life. I am proud to be a citizen of this amazing country!

Table of Contents

ACKNOWLEDGMENTS

Without the inspiration of the following people, this book would not be possible. I owe a lot to all of them. The impact which you all had on my life and my personal development has been incredible, and I will always be grateful for that.

1. **Pa Joof – The man with personality, business acumen and superb work ethic.**

I thank Mr. Pa Joof for his extraordinary support during the whole process of writing this book. His values and the values of his family are always a source of inspiration for me and had a great impact on my career and life. His ambition to impact the lives of people in Africa and the ability to lead is something which I always look forward too as an example.

Website: www.pajoof.com

2. **Marc Jospitre – His sales techniques are unconventional and work. The person who helped me in becoming a better version of myself. He is always a source of inspiration who keeps the burning desire to excel alive.**

I have been inspired by the unique coaching style of Mr. Marc Jospitre. His sales acumen reflects in his results and he is one of the very few people who have the ability to elaborate the most complicated concepts in a way that they are understandable and intuitive. His work ethic, commitment and perseverance and be gauged from the fact that he is one of the best consultants for Mr. Bob proctor who is the pioneer of personal development space. I firmly believe that he will realise his vision and impact billions, and, in this way, he will leave a legacy which very people ever will.

Website: https://www.marcjospitre.com/

3. **Tiji Thomas – The sales guru who gave me the inspiration to write this book. I will run out of words but won't be able to return the favours.**

I will like to thank Mr. Tiji Thomas for the value which he gave me and many others on social media. Tiji Thomas is an embodiment of courtesy and generosity and that truly reflects in his sales closing style. The value which he gives on social media is superb. I have been following him for a long time and had the privilege to have a conversation with him. His sales techniques and methodologies resonate with me and it was nice to see the parallel in our sales closing styles. I firmly believe that Mr. Tiji Thomas is one of the most impactful people when it comes to integrity-based sales closing!

Website: https://tijithomas.com/

4. **Christian Moser – The energy and the passion which radiates from your words is unmatched. Keep on creating the impact and follow your vision. You are awesome.**

Mr. Christian Moser has helped people in Germany and around the globe in sales and in this way, he has helped them to realise their full potential. His energy and drive are evident from the fact that he is always thinking about ways to constantly impact people around the globe.

Website: http://thechristianmoser.com/

Also, by Subayal:

1. *If you are unable to close on your idea, product or service, you cannot help people.*

2. *For every client that I am unable to close, I am implicitly depriving them and their family of a bright future!*

3. *Closing is a skill which anyone can learn, and mastery comes with practice, experience and time!*

Closing With
Clarity, Conviction and
Confidence.

SECTION 1:

INTRODUCTION

CHAPTER 1

Overview and Preliminary Concepts

The role of this book is to help you master the art of sales closing in order to become a top-notch salesperson in any industry. This book approaches the art of sales closing from a trust-centric and problem-solving perspective. The main aim of this book is to teach you the skills, tools and techniques that will help you to avoid approaching a sales conversations and meetings in a self-centred way. By doing so, you won't focus on product features or compare your services to the competitors and rather focus on solving the problem of your prospect. This approach will help in identifying the gap between the current state goals of the prospect and dig deep into their emotional pains and desires. Therefore, the book will help you in eradicating the habits and challenges of conventional salesmen by doing the following:

1. **Avoid closing sales in a traditional, boring, feature centric and self-centred way.**

2. **Avoid getting stuck in a loop of self-sabotage and stagnation, which is primarily because of the wrong mindset and identity "which one has chosen for oneself."**

3. **Excel as a salesperson in lucrative and fast-growing sectors such as Personal Development and Real Estate, where the transaction sizes can range from thousands to millions of USD. In this way, you will be able to leverage the growth of these sectors and secure your financial future.**

4. **Learn why the philosophy that customers are more concerned with features and technical details is flawed to its core.**

5. Get rid of the fundamental beliefs hardcoded in the minds of many salespeople that a sales closing call is competition-centric, or product features-centric.

6. Overcome the need to convince the prospect that your product or service is better than competitors or alternatives. At higher price points, it is all about the desires and wants of prospects and not needs.

7. Understand that customers mostly pay a premium for the experience and feelings associated with that, and not for the functionality and utility. This will be life-changing for you and your family. On the other hand, you can go broke by selling cheap products or services to people with lower income. That is why the book focuses on mastering sales closing of high-end products and services.

You must keep in mind:

In order to become a top-notch salesperson, you must remember that the prospects have a problem or "problems" and there exists an opposite of it, their "vision" or "dream," which they want desperately or crave. And that is why they are on a call with you. So never think that your product or service lacks value. Even if it is not valuable to you, prospects see value in it. You must keep in mind.

1. Prospects don't have time to be on call with you just to have a conversation with you or meet you without any reason. So, they have a problem which is worth solving for them, and they value their time. If they don't value their time, it means that they don't deserve to be your clients in the first place.

2. Clients from hell are never good for your business, reputation and in most cases well-being. Perhaps you did, are doing or want to do business with a bad client because you are operating from a scarcity mindset

and you haven't installed the proper mindset yet.

3. Bad clients are bad for your reputation too. Which is not a good thing in the long run for your brand.

4. The main reason due to which you are doing it is the lack of abundance and proper mindset and that is why 3 whole sections are dedicated to mindset training in this course.

Sale as a transfer of energy:

In order to close sales like a top-notch salesperson, you must understand that a sale is a transfer of energy and therefore, you must remember these points:

1. You must radiate belief, passion, conviction and commitment in your voice.

2. Trust is the precursor to any business transaction. The prospect buys you before purchasing your product your service. That is why "rapport" comes first which is important to develop the trust.

3. At subconscious level, they will know if you:

   i.   Don't have belief.
   ii. Don't have conviction.
   iii. Don't have commitment.

In short, here is what I have learned after decades of experience in sales closing:

You simply cannot escape your inner world. You will always radiate your inner energy in your tonality and voice.

—Subayal

They simply won't purchase your product or service if your inner world is not in alignment with *what you say* and *how you say it*. The misalignment will be sensed by the prospect and they won't purchase your service as a result.

Connect to serve with right intent.

You must make them feel that you will help them overcome challenges in their life by being confident and certain about your service. Always conduct or execute a closing call with full confidence; whether they will purchase your service or not is not a problem. The reason is that everyone cannot be a right fit for your service, and everyone can't have a desire to overcoming their obstacles. Here are the salient points which one must remember about sales closing:

1. **Sales closing does not imply shutting the door or closing of something. Closing is in fact the beginning of a new transformation or change for the prospect; for example, introducing new business processes, forging new marketing strategy, or shaping a new personal development service for their audience.**

2. **Your goal is to get the right information and emotion out of a prospect. Notice the joy, unhappiness, or lack of fulfilment from the facial expressions of the prospects to better understand their needs and find out if your service or product is a right fit for them.**

3. Your job is to take a prospect from a sceptical frame of mind to a buyer's frame of mind if you know that your service or product will serve them. You must do it FOR THEM and do it with an INTENT TO SERVE. You must have the best interest of the prospect at hand.

4. Therefore, as a closer, all you need to do is to MASTER the art of helping the prospect. This means that you have to help them make a shift from a sceptical mindset to a Buyer's mindset:

Therefore, with belief, conviction and their best interests at heart, you take them from a mindset of no trust, no need, no urgency, no help and no support to trust, need to make a change, and urgency, and provide them with help and support. In this way, they can start the journey and start a process of transformation or change that will ultimately help them solve their problems.

Sceptical Mindset   Buyer's Mindset

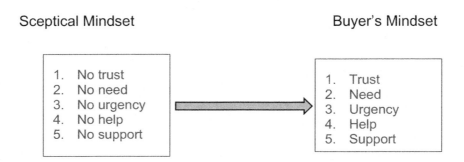

As a closer, you have to be comfortable with the uncomfortable. In this way, you will be able to connect to serve and influence people so that they can do what is right for them. Your intent should be helping the people get what they need so that they don't suffer anymore. In order to do that, you have to invoke the right emotions and also feel the emotions of the prospects as they experience them during a sales conversation. That requires the right observation skills and will help you to take the sales closing conversation in the right direction. During a sales conversation, you have to constantly evaluate and ask yourself: Are you taking the prospects deep into their feelings, or helping them realise what actually lies in their subconscious mind? That is important, because people buy with their heart, emotions or what is lying in their subconscious mind.

You also must understand that if you are able to penetrate the prospect's defences, you can help them overcome their challenges. So, during a sales conversation, you have to observe and make notes. In short, sales closing is an art of adapting your behaviour to help your prospects make the right decisions. By doing so, they can get the results which will impact their lives positively. If you are approaching sales closing with a purely logical or unemotional perspective, you will never get great results. If you are unable to close the sales, the prospects stay where they are, and their lives don't change. Also, you won't be able to create any impact, and you will stay where you are in your career and financially. In short, not closing prospects is a lose-lose situation both for you and for them, and both you and your prospect stay where you are.

Therefore, this book follows a very different approach which contrasts with the traditional sales books and focuses first on the mindset, unconventional wisdom, and underlying mechanics of a sales conversation. Only once the right mindset and beliefs are installed do we apply the most effective and proven strategies, tools and techniques for closing high-ticket sales. This process will transform you into a top-notch closer and you will be able to operate with confidence, conviction and absolute clarity.

Who is this book for?

This book is for both experienced sale closers and people from other backgrounds with no experience in sales whatsoever. If you already have a sales career, this book will give you a fresh perspective, challenge your existing beliefs, improve your mindset, install new beliefs and give you tools and techniques which will boost your sales career tremendously. Also, this book can take complete newbies and help them start their sales closing career with a concrete foundation and unconventional knowledge. This book also provides the framework for continually increasing your confidence and competence so that anyone with any level of prior sales experience can transform into a top-notch sale closer.

How this book is organized

We start by elaborating the power of mindset, identity and other essential concepts in sufficient depth so that these concepts can refine and enhance your closing skills, and you can start closing sales with confidence and conviction. I have found that these concepts are neglected, described vaguely or introduced at the surface in many sales books, which motivated me to write this book. This book is the only book which you will ever need to excel as a successful salesperson by closing more sales.

The knowledge described in section 3, 4 and 5 elaborates the beliefs and mindset that will give you conviction and confidence. This will motivate you to remain consistent and committed, and in this way, enhance your results when you apply the strategies, skills, and techniques presented in the last three sections, sections 6 to 8. Therefore, we first work on your inner world in the first three sections, which will manifest itself in the form of brilliant performance when you make use of the strategies and tools in the last three sections.

There are many perspectives, realities and concepts which I have described in this book and once you understand these concepts thoroughly, you will thrive as a salesperson by closing more sales in any industry.

Why closing conversation is indispensable

The sales closing has emerged as the most critical skill for salespersons because of the way technologies have evolved and their impact on the way we communicate, conduct business and socialize. The communities are formed online on platforms such as Facebook while applications such as Skype, Zoom and WhatsApp have changed the way we hold business meetings. In the last eight years, I have met the majority of my clients online before I physically met them. In most cases, they had already started a business relationship with me months before.

That converges to one significant point; the physical business meetings are becoming a thing of the past while the online meetings with prospects and clients are dominating the business world. Therefore, to survive in this new era, one must master the art of closing conversation since the majority of businesses are going online. As a result, the majority of prospects are converted into clients over a phone call. In this book, the term "phone call" refers to any sales closing conversation "audio or video meeting" that is done via a software application or mobile phone. Here are some of the most important reasons due to which closing on the phone has emerged as a critical skill which is in high demand.

You can have online video meetings with clients and make use of body language, tonality as well as words for online sales closing conversations. The exact same principles and techniques can be applied to the physical meetings too.

You can absolutely apply the same techniques to the physical meetings if you are working in a sector such as Real Estate. The methodologies and techniques taught in this course are agnostic to the industry and can be applied in any sector. Here are the some of the key reasons which make it an important and high in-demand skill.

1. E-Commerce "Selling products or services online"

As you can see, internet technologies have made it easy to sell products and services globally. You can be in one country, and you can sell your products and services in any other country across the globe. That makes it essential for many business owners to set up a team of sale closers who can close the sales over the phone.

2. Global clients

Furthermore, the influencers, experts, manufactures and multinationals are now targeting clients globally via their services and products to leverage the global demand. Many times, the influencers need closers in the local time zones of prospects so that they can work in the daytime during business hours. Also, the fact that they have a better understanding of the culture and can communicate in the local language helps them develop rapport quickly. This helps in building trust faster and increases the closing rate.

3. Social media and targeted advertising

The social media has made it easier to advertise to the right audience around the globe with the click of a button. Nowadays, a business owner can reach the audience via ads in any country. In this way, the leads are funnelled to the calendars of closers where they can get on the phone with them, close the sale and convert prospects into clients.

4. Global demand

Nowadays, people have the opportunity to avail the services of best coaches, mentors, fitness and domain exerts in any country.

Therefore, they are hungry to get in touch with their sales staff to avail the best possible services in the market for improving their lives, skills and businesses. Hence, in most cases, the prospects book a call with one of the closers on their sales team to have a conversation with them before becoming customers. Many people want to work with the best people, learn from the best people and get mentorship from the best people irrespective of where they live. They are more concerned about the quality, exclusivity and value proposition rather than the geographic location. Internet has made it possible to access most services, and order majority of physical products from any part of the world over the internet. Therefore, nowadays purchasing decisions are made over the phone because people don't have the time to go on a plane to another country to meet the experts face to face.

5. Limited time of influencers

Also, the experts don't have the time to meet hundreds or thousands of clients in person via a face to face meetings. Also, purchasing a flight ticket, booking a hotel, leaving their work and taking time off work can cost prospects a lot. Hence, closing over the phone is becoming more and more common. Therefore, in many cases, the clients are incentivized to get on a phone call with a salesperson and figure out if the service or product is a right fit for them.

6. Need of clarity and knowing if it is a right fit

For most of the high-ticket services, the customers need clarity so that they know that the product or service will help them overcome their challenges. Hence, to make a well-informed decision, they need to get on the phone with someone in order to discuss their challenges and wants. For that reason, they need to get on the phone for having a conversation with a salesperson whose role is to close the sale.

7. Desire to solve Global problems instead of local ones

Nowadays, the businesses, influencers and experts try to solve global problems instead of the local problems. The main motive behind that is to leave a legacy by solving issues that transcend the borders of nations. The trade barriers are diminishing, and at the same time, firms like Amazon, PayPal, Facebook, YouTube and LinkedIn have made it possible to reach out to the target audience via ads. To convert the prospects into clients, business owners usually need sale closers from different courtiers in different time zones to convert prospects into clients. It would be best if you learn the art of sales closing to generate a good stable income at this time.

CHAPTER 2

The most important thing is your "Why"

In this chapter, the main aim is to facilitate you in making a concrete decision with absolute clarity. Once you have the conviction that sales closing is crucial skill for you to learn, you will happily and intentionally immerse yourself into the information presented in this book. Once that happens, learning this new skill will become effortless, joyful and fulfilling.

Whenever you want to master a new skill, the most important thing is to have the absolute conviction that the new skill must be mastered because it will serve you. If you're going to learn it for fun, as a part-time gig or as a hobby, you won't be able to master it. Your skills will remain average because you won't have strong underlying reasons for learning the craft. Therefore, you must ask yourself:

Question 1: Why should you master this new skill?

Remember the wording used in the question. It is "master," not "learn." So, if you don't know a clear answer to this question, it means that you don't want the "mastery" of new skill badly enough. You must have the belief that this skill will serve you. If you know your motivation for acquiring the new skill, you will practice, learn, and apply the skill. Also, your emotional energy will compel you to take action, persevere, and overcome obstacles as you master the skill. You will feel satisfied, fulfilled and practicing it will become pure joy. If you don't know the answer to this question, you will not commit, persevere and excel in that area. Therefore, the first question can rephrase the question as:

Question 2: Why must you become a top-notch closer?

The reason for these two questions is that your motivation might be different than mine. I applied closing skills to close sales over the phone and closing personal development sales. Personal development sales are more aligned with my vision, mission and, events in my life and my story. Your interests, motivation and industry might be different for example, in other words:

1. **You might be motivated to apply it in real estate, the automotive industry or any other area of your choice.**

2. **Your circumstances are different than mine.**

3. **Your future vision might be different than mine.**

4. **Your needs and priorities might be different**

In the next chapter, I will tell you my why, meaning: Why did I started closing sales for influencers? Why am I happy to close sales on phone or Skype (video or audio meetings depending on preferences of clients)? That will help you formulate your own "why."

Please note that the concepts and theories in this training are applicable in any industry and you can apply this knowledge at any stage of your sales career, even as a complete newbie.

CHAPTER 3

My "Why": Why I started closing for influencers over phone

The goal of this chapter is to help you form your own "Why." Here are the questions which can help you develop your "why" and helped me form mine.

Reason 1: Personal reasons

Here are the reasons which formed my Why:

1. I value my family time a lot and I wanted to spend more time with my family.

2. I don't like to travel each day to work (in many cases, it can take two hours each day to commute to work).

3. It saves me the time which I would have spent commuting to the office. I can allocate that time to my other projects.

4. It is a transferrable skill and it can improve my negotiation skills which I can apply in other areas of my life.

5. I can make a good income from my home.

6. I can exercise more and focus on more on my health.

Reason 2: Evolution of technologies and impact of e-commerce/internet

These points will help you discover the key benefits of sales closing, and these benefits might be congruent with what you have always desired in your life. All of this will help you shape your own "why," which is the ultimate goal of this section. Here are the eight key points.

1. Rapidly evolving technologies:

Many repetitive jobs will disappear. They will be replaced by machines that are forged by technologies like the Internet of Things, Artificial Intelligence and Robotics. Therefore, if you think that you can retire by sitting on a chair in a superstore by just scanning barcodes over and over again each day, forget it. It is a delusional thought. Already, in many stores, automated checkout machines are installed which do not require any human involvement. The banking sector is going through a revolution. Online banks are rapidly replacing the brick and mortar banks which require many times less workforce and provide many of the same services which a brick and mortar bank offers. The introduction of blockchain technology to manage cross border value transfer as well as services like TransferWise are eroding the profits of banks. The repetitive tasks in every industry will soon be replaced by more optimal solutions enabled by novel technologies to optimize costs and improve efficiency. Hence, you have to act fast. The world is evolving at a rapid speed, and if you don't upgrade your skills according to the needs of the market, you will probably lose your job and be caught off-guard. This is precisely the time when you can leverage this unique opportunity in a market which is hungry for good closers. Closing is a skill which can make you good money from anywhere in the world with just a smartphone. Therefore, this skill can save you from upcoming financial stress and provide you with good cash flow for decades to come. It is your hedge against the changing global technological landscape where industries are rapidly inducting new technologies to improve their bottom line. A robot or machine does not need a pension, does not require medical care, has a warranty and can work in the same way consistently for a much longer duration than a human. Also, it is easily replaceable, does not argue, does not have any attitude problems (robots do not have emotions) and most of all, can work 24/7. Surely robots need maintenance, software upgrades and replacement, but you will agree that the headaches are way less.

2. Location agnostic lifestyle:

Who wants to wake up at 6:00 AM or 7:00 AM in his hometown, go to a major city like Helsinki, Stockholm or London on a train, do a 9:00 AM to 5:00 PM job, then come back home at 7:00 PM or 8:00 PM? And also earn (most likely) in the range of three to six thousand EUR or GBP per month with taxes. Why would you not get up in the morning, turn on the computer, do some roleplays, check the calendar, talk to the inbound leads or pre-determined outbound leads and call them to close the sales? The customer details are already available, since they have either been to an event, watched the webinar or attended to a preliminary training. In most cases, the prospects view an ad of the offered service online and are interested. The prospects fill out a form and provide their telephone number during their journey through the sales funnel before calling you. Therefore, there are no headaches associated with cold calling. Since they have some information about the service or product, your main focus is to understand their current challenges and see if your service is the right fit for them. Your aim is to ask them the right questions to understand the impact of the problem on their business or life. After asking questions, if you find that it is a good fit, you close the sale.

3. Well-being and work-life balance:

You can exercise during the time it takes you to travel to the office in the morning and come back, and in this way, you can be fitter and healthier. You can work longer, you can work during times that suit you, you can have vacations when you want and as long as you want. Also, you can work on your holidays, and you can enjoy your mornings and afternoons with your kids. You are in charge of your time and dictate the lifestyle which you want to have. This feeling of control and freedom is in itself worth mastering this skill.

4. The millennials are glued to computer screens:

Millennials and younger people fuel the demand for this skill. They find it hard to have meaningful conversations and cannot communicate effectively over the phone. Thanks to Steve Jobs, the iPhone gave rise to the touch screen mobile phones. These devices have given humans the ability to interact without talking to each other face to face or verbally. Nowadays, millennials and younger people are more eager to add people on Facebook, and if you tell them to call someone, they won't do it. Talking to someone else directly on the phone is just too stressful and uncomfortable for them. The online video games played on phones and laptops, YouTube and social media have glued the younger generation to the screens. It has reduced their direct "verbal" and "face to face" social interaction to such an extent that this hungry market is craving for good closers. One can leverage this shortcoming of the younger generation and quickly become an elite salesperson by mastering the art of sales closing, since the level of skill needed to do a good enough job as a closer and start in this area is just not that high. The bar is too low since the art of communication is vanishing, and people cannot connect as easily to others as they could only two decades back.

5. Low risk:

All that you need for closing is a phone or a computer along with a set of headphones. All of these you probably already have. You don't need to resign from your job suddenly; you can start closing on weekends and in evenings in the beginning. With time, your sales closing skill will become better, and income will grow. When you see that you can replace much of your salary by closing commissions, you can resign your job. Or, if possible, you can reduce your working hours gradually before shifting to full time closing. You don't need to invest heavily to set up a sales closing business. Unlike a traditional company, when things are not working out well, there is a financial cost attached to poor performance.

In closing, you learn something from the failed closing calls and that learning experience in itself compensates for the 30-40 minutes of your call. You can record your call and learn from it too. You don't lose a single penny on running costs since you can close sales from the comfort of your home. You are making money by leveraging the success of the business owner for who are your clients. However, keep in mind that sales closing does need commitment and hard work. So, it is a skill that is mastered via persistent action, and you do need to work for 7-10 hours a day in most cases to make a decent living. However, the good thing is that you learn with every call and the more calls you make, the more you grow, and the more you eventually earn.

6. Global Impact:

As a sale closer, you will most likely be talking to clients from different countries. Therefore, you will interact with people from different cultures, which will enhance your cross-cultural competence. This will also help you understand what drives people and how people think, why people reach certain conclusions and say certain words, and what gets people emotionally involved. This skill will help you in many areas of your life and enable you to achieve your goals. It can help you close people on your ideas, raise capital for your business, or help you in getting a much lower interest rate on your mortgage. You will know how to figure out the motivation of people who are selling their business or house and negotiate well. In this way, this one skill will make you decent money and positively impact different areas of your life. If you become an influencer or business owner in the future, you will quickly understand the emotional impact of your words and tonality. In this way, it will help you build rapport with others and connect with the audience.

7. Transferable skill:

Closing is everywhere. When you buy an existing business and want to convince a bank for a loan, you need to close them. Also, when you want to buy a house, you can always use your closing skills to get a better deal. When you understand the concepts explained in this book, you will know why people make particular purchasing decisions, and what role emotions play in them. You can apply your closing skills in any industry ranging from real estate to personal development. In this way, you can work in the industry of your choice. Furthermore, the closing skill will also help you in understanding the motives of other people when they talk about brands or specific places. This can help you create your personal brand and speak to the heart of your audience.

8. Diminishing need for physical interaction:

Meritocracy is the name of the game, and the customers always want to find the right services which will solve their problem irrespective of the geographic location. That is why a majority of services can be now found online (except for some services such as medical care, where in most cases the clients have to meet a physician in person). Also, products can be shipped globally.

Therefore, the need for closers is increasing. They understand the challenges of customers, qualify them and educate them about their products and services. In this way, they facilitate prospects in making better purchasing decisions. Also, the extent to which people base their decisions on social proof is evident from the success of Amazon and eBay. Two decades back, people did not trust online stores, but now in many counties people purchase most things online. All of this is due to the connected world where people share information, interact, buy, and sell online via platforms such as Facebook, LinkedIn, Twitter, YouTube, eBay and Amazon. Hence, for high-end services and products, prospects are eager to book a call with you to learn more about the products or services and make a better purchasing decision. Your job as a sale closer is to facilitate that process by helping them realise and understand if the product is a right fit for them. In this way, they can make a better buying decision.

CHAPTER 4

Exercise: Define Your Why

Now you already know my "Why" and how I formed it. In this chapter, I have composed a set of questions which will help you in coming up with your own "Why." This is fundamentally important because it will keep you focused and motivated as you master the art of sales closing. Here are the questions:

1. How will this skill help you achieve the lifestyle that you want?

2. Why is the right time to master the Sales Closing now?

3. Why is it essential for improving my lifestyle?

4. Is it the lowest risk option to safeguard your financial future?

5. Is it one of the best ways to impact people globally?

6. Is this skill transferable?

7. Can I work from anywhere in the world and travel to beautiful places while working?

8. Why is "conversation" getting more and more important in sales closing?

9. How can I leverage the diminishing trend of decreasing desire for physical meetings with business owners and experts?

I strongly recommend that you write answers to these questions on paper in your own words and revise them a few times. Think what else you want to achieve by acquiring this skill. The more solid and clear your answers, the more motivated you will be and the more focused you will remain as you go through the ups and downs in your sales career.

It is not about the circumstances; it is about the way we respond to them. If I can do it, so can you.

—Subayal

SECTION 2:

SIX STEPS TO BECOME A TOP-NOTCH SALESPERSON IN ANY INDUSTRY!

CHAPTER 5

Why Most Salespersons Get Average Results

My success in this area stems from the fact that I mastered the art of sales closing by working on all aspects of this craft. Over the course of your career, you will see many business owners who want you to read out a word by word script to the prospects, but that never works. The majority of entrepreneurs, business development professionals, salespersons, and sales managers actually have bad or average sales closing skills. If that wasn't the case, the sales gurus would instead emphasize more on the underlying foundations which help a top-notch salesperson to have outstanding sales closing skills. Instead, they only focus on the scripts, techniques and tools.

The problem is that most salespersons don't:

1. **Have the conviction that the product or service which they are selling works.**

2. **Have the conviction that "closing is not something that you do to a prospect but for the prospect".**

3. **Have the conviction that people might have a different perception of value which might contradict with your own perception of value.**

4. **Liberate themselves from projecting their value onto prospects.**

5. **Understand the power of tonality.**

6. Understand that doing the opposite of what a stereotypical salesman does is better.

7. Understand that selling high-end services and products is better.

8. Understand that transaction size matters.

If you don't get rid of these problems,

"You will never be able to become a top-notch closer!"

—Subayal

The reason is that:

Your outer world is always a reflection of your inner world and the prison of mind is the hardest prison to escape. Your inner beliefs and mindset will project during a sales meeting and your prospects will sense it.

—Subayal

In the next chapter, I will describe the exact tested and proven 6 step process that made me and many of my friends, students and colleagues into top-notch closers.

CHAPTER 6

The Proven 6 Step Process to Become A Top-Notch Closer

If you don't mitigate the 8 problems mentioned in previous chapter, you still might achieve some success and get satisfactory results but won't become a top-notch salesperson. Becoming an expert in this area requires a thorough understanding of the way these key elements play a fundamental role in mastering the craft. I know it because I have lived it, I have learned it the hard way, and I have seen many experienced salespersons getting frustrated and leaving their sales careers because they cannot close the sales with confidence and conviction. On the other hand, I have seen newbies with no sales experience excelling in this area and developing a strong foundation by applying the knowledge mentioned in this book.

One can develop strong sales closing skills by understanding the concepts described in the first three sections of the book. These concepts will give you the conviction and clarity that will motivate you to remain committed and consistent as you apply the tools, techniques and strategies in the remainder of the book. Without the conviction and clarity, the strategies and tools will not take you further since you will quickly lose interest and get distracted.

While I was learning the art of sales closing to become a successful salesperson, I observed that my journey of mastering this art could be divided into six steps, as shown in Error! Reference source not found..

The first two sections provide the foundation and overview of the way this book is organized. In the last 6 sections, we cover the 6-step process which is required to forge you into a top-notch closer. Each of these sections cover the knowledge required to successfully complete one step in the six-step process. Hence, each section corresponds to one step of your journey.

First two Sections = foundation and overview of the way this book is organized.

Last 6 sections = the 6-step process which is required to forge you into a top-notch closer.

I have seen many of my colleagues and friends who used this 6-step process and achieved tremendous results within a few weeks—even those who started as complete newbies. If you follow and apply the concepts and techniques described in these sections, I am confident that you will master the art of sale closing which will help you become a top-notch salesperson. Once the solid foundation is formed in the first three steps, you can start learning the skills and strategies, and master them by via the techniques mentioned in **section 8** (Step six of the six step process).

As shown in Figure 1, each of the six steps required for mastering the art of sales closing and becoming a top-notch salesperson are mentioned in the corresponding sections. The first three steps focus on the mindset, identity and psychology and define the first milestone. After achieving this milestone, you will have the mindset, beliefs and identity that will enable you to operate like a top-notch closer. The last three steps focus on the strategies, tools and techniques and define the second and last milestone. After this milestone, you will be equipped with all the knowledge you need to confidently start a sales closing career or take your sales career to the next level. Your skills and competence will grow with time as you practice and apply this knowledge.

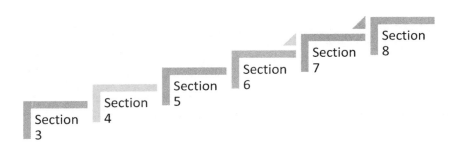

FIGURE 1: THE SIX STEPS REQUIRED FOR BECOMING A TOP-NOTCH CLOSER ARE MENTIONED IN THE CORRESPONDING SECTION. THE FIRST THREE STEPS FOCUS ON THE MINDSET, IDENTITY AND PSYCHOLOGY AND DEFINE THE FIRST MILESTONE. THE LAST THREE STEPS FOCUS ON THE STRATEGIES, TOOLS AND TECHNIQUES AND DEFINE THE LAST MILESTONE.

If you follow these steps, your growth as a salesperson will increase tremendously since you will be able to close more sales. To master the art of sale closing, you have to maintain laser-sharp focus, iron-hard conviction and unshakeable core beliefs. By the end of the book, the 8 problems mentioned in previous chapter will be mitigated, and this in-demand and high-income skill of sale closing will be mastered. As you go through the chapters of the book, in each of the six sections, your beliefs will be challenged, and your ideas about sales and sale closing will be replaced and taken over by new ones. This transformation will put you on a path of continuous growth, which will take you to your ultimate destiny, i.e., becoming a top-notch salesperson with brilliant closing skills in your industry. Those who are new to this game or who have never

44

closed a single sale before, I congratulate the most since they are going to learn this art the right way from the start. The experienced salespersons should be happy too, since this book will help them unlearn tons of strategies and shatter their current beliefs which don't serve them. This book will help them learn new effective strategies and enable them to replace old beliefs with new ones. These new beliefs, tested strategies, and in-depth knowledge will take their sales careers to a new level in a much shorter time frame.

So, congratulations ladies and gentlemen, we are now done with the overview of the book. We will now start the exact 6 step process which took me from a newbie and introverted scientist to an elite salesperson who successfully closed industrial partners of industrial consortium for multi-million EUR projects and is currently working with the most renowned influencers in the personal development area.

Each of the following sections covers one step in your journey which will transform you into a top-notch closer.

So, are you excited?

Are you fired up?

Ready to go?

If yes, let us start off and master the art of sales closing which will help you tremendously throughout your career.

Our success is not determined by our circumstances but by the way we respond to them. If I can do it, so can you.

—Subayal

SECTION 3:

STEP 1: WHAT IT TAKES TO BECOME A TOP-NOTCH CLOSER

CHAPTER 7

Can You Become a Top-Notch Closer?

Over the years, many of my colleagues, friends and fellow salespersons have asked me countless times about my journey and the way I overcame self-doubt, fear and challenges associated with learning a new skill, mastering it and creating a powerful personal brand. Every time, when I listen to these questions, it reminds me the start of my own journey. I have to admit that it wasn't easy. Also, I know that these questions have a lot to do with our mindset, our beliefs, and our current skill level. Let me go through these questions and answer them.

The answer to the question: Can I become a top-notch closer? is: Yes, you can become a top-notch closer, anyone can become a top-notch closer, and you can become a top-notch closer irrespective of your background and circumstances. However, this is only possible if you choose the identity of a closer for yourself and work on your mindset. Once you do that, you will be able to effectively apply the strategies and techniques described in the 6th, 7th and 8th sections of the book. Therefore, it is imperative to grasp the concepts described in the first three steps of the book which describe the power of mindset and identity.

I have observed during my career as a sales mentor and coach that many salespersons get stuck in the stagnation loop, where the wrong mindset and identity is at play in the background. This results in a low closing rate for salespersons because they have not embraced the identity of an elite salesperson who can close sales with conviction and confidence. The average performance results in self-doubt, and the salesperson starts to look for reasons to validate his average performance. As a result, it causes stress, non-fulfilment and lack of self-belief. This further consolidates the thoughts and patterns which strengthen the wrong mindset and feed the wrong identity, making it more and more deeply rooted in the subconscious mind, and this vicious cycle repeats as shown in Figure 2.

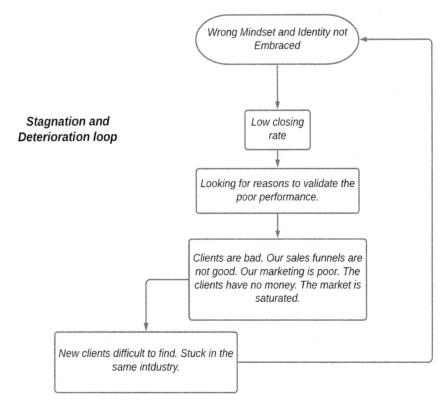

FIGURE 2: THE STAGNATION AND DETERIORATION LOOP

Contrary to the stagnation and deterioration loop is "the growth loop" as shown in Figure 3. In this case, a person's positive mindset and the right identity results in great results. This results in positivity, fulfillment and joy. This further consolidates the positive mindset and identity, and the cycle repeats as shown in Figure 3.

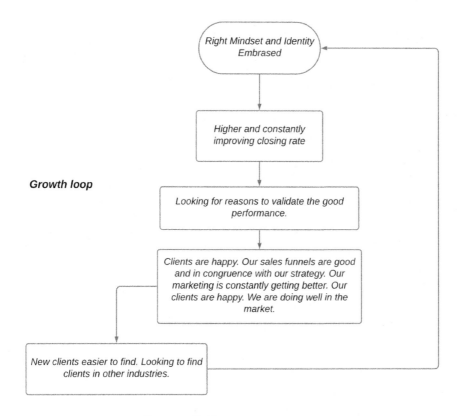

Growth loop

FIGURE 3: THE GROWTH LOOP

In the last step of the framework, we will describe the proven system which you can apply to shatter the barriers which are holding you back if you are stuck in the so-called "stagnation and deterioration loop." The frameworks described in last step will help you make a switch from the "stagnation and deterioration loop" to the "growth loop". That will help you turbo charge your inner strength and reach your goals much faster.

CHAPTER 8

The Myth of Natural Talent

The myth that someone has natural talent for sales closing is fundamentally flawed. It is all about the identity which one has embraced. I hear people saying, "Tiger Woods is so natural." What they don't know is that he used to spend countless hours practicing when his peers were gone. They wanted to become "good enough" players. They had embraced that mediocrity mindset. On the other hand, Tiger Woods had embraced the identity of "the best player in the world" for himself. To remain congruent with his identity, he had to practice, he had to push himself to go the extra mile. He had to be resourceful and overcome all the obstacles to reach his destiny. You see, the majority of people say, "he or she is so natural" as if the person was born with some unique genes. I simply cannot stand these people. People remain in their current state because they focus on the current state of successful people.

The main problem is that people are mostly focused on the current state of successful people, and don't consider the humble beginnings, initial obstacles, struggles, uncertainty and setbacks that they encountered all along the way. This narrow-sighted view gives them reasons to remain confined to their current state. Due to this, they remain stuck and don't take any action to move towards their goals.

This keeps them confined to their comfort zone, and they justify that by believing that they can't be like the other person since his or her skills and competencies are naturally way better. That is very problematic, because one's comfort zone is one's income zone. Therefore, the abundance and fulfilment come when one disrupts, overcomes and shatters the walls of one's comfort zone, which is forged by one's wrong beliefs. You must obliterate the fears and doubts associated with uncertainty that you might face when you move out of your comfort zone. When you do that and take action, you will be unstoppable, and you will be able to achieve anything you want.

> *"Things that are external to us cannot stop us from achieving our goals, but things inside us can definitely do that.*
>
> *—Subayal*

Also,

> *"Your environment and others are not the problem, but the way you perceive them is a problem and is holding you back!"*
>
> *—Subayal*

If you look at life as a growth-centric experience, you will outgrow your current state. It would be best if you don't compare yourself to the best people in the area of sales and instead focus on your growth. You have to realise that the "best salespersons" or top-notch professionals in any field are just at another stage in their growth. They were once at the same level of growth as you are now, and maybe even below that at some point in their career. So, if they can grow to that level by remaining committed to their profession, so can you. You are actually at an advantage since you can learn from the struggles and setbacks that they encountered during their journey of growth and do things in a more optimal way than them.

Are you convinced?

If you are now convinced that it is really the case, does it really matter that you just started your sales career, or you want to take your sales career to the next level? The clear answer is no, everyone starts at some point, and you are doing the same. So, the whole point of this discussion is that you should have a concrete belief in yourself and look at life as a "growth-centric experience."

CHAPTER 9

Environment and Commitment

You must remember that you might love your parents, relatives and friends a lot, but you might have different goals, ambitions or desires. Meaning, you might not want their life, even though you love them. Remember that you should never take advice from a person whose life you don't want, since that will put you on a track which leads to the life they are living. Hence, you should only take advice from people whose life you want. I have no idea as to how many global enterprises, innovative ideas and business empires were ruined due to the advice given for free by relatives and closest friends. Go and find a circle of friends whose goals are congruent with yours and whose life you want. In this way, you will start operating at the same frequency as them.

I am a realist and I will not sugar coat anything by being hyper optimistic. You should have the conviction that that life is not always easy but does not mean in that you should give up hope and. Remember that if you will attempt easy things, you will not violate your comfort zone and you will have a hard life. On the contrary, if you will do what's hard, you will have a life of abundance and fulfilment.

Countless studies have revealed that laziness is mostly a result of low levels of motivation which is in turn caused due to distractions, over-stimulation or excessive impulses. Therefore, staying focused and committed are the key to your success. You should be cautiously aware of procrastination and laziness because both can result in average or bad results which can eventually decapitate the power of will. Commitment has a formal structure and you must operate like a professional to achieve your goals. Section 8 "last step of the book", I have laid out a well-defined approach which anyone can use to achieve anything in life by staying focused and disciplined. This framework will help you improve your skills and give you a slight edge over your peers which will help you in staying at the top of your game.

Remember that in life you might not get what you want but you will most probably get what you deserve. Even though no one can point out the exact and precise causes of a person's failure. But I can say with absolute conviction that negativity, bad self-image and victim mentality will never allow you to live the life your dreams which you crave. We can never outgrow our self-image and our success is mostly a result of our peer group and environment. Therefore, to excel in any area of your life, you must develop the proper mindset, habits, and skills which will help you in becoming a top-notch expert in your area. You must:

i. **You must accept the struggles as part of your growth.**

ii. **You should have a brilliant work ethic so that you can persevere effortlessly.**

iii. **You should only surround yourself with like-minded individuals. These are the people whose lives you want.**

iv. **Take full ownership of your actions and take imperfect action daily.**

v. **Always measure your wins and losses because whatever gets measures gets improved.**

vi. **You should always be passionate about your goals. Also, you should always be obsessed with the outcome of your efforts.**

Therefore, you must take control of your environment and make sure that you won't let other people's opinions to determine the outcome of your efforts. You should learn from people those who have been where you want to go and crave the information which you can apply for accelerating your results. This will help you in merging your willpower with well-defined action steps which will take you to your destination.

CHAPTER 10

Role of closing in my career

During my career, I made a successful transition from an expert in computer systems to a top-notch closer. This transition took over a decade and was gradual and full of stressful moments. Also, during my career, my closing skills evolved as I achieved different objectives in my career. Also, my closing skills helped me achieve several objectives, as shown in Figure 4. While achieving these objectives, I would not only put my closing skills to test but also learn new closing techniques and strategies which would help me enhance my closing competencies. As you can observe, throughout my career, I was open to change, I was free to learn new skills, and I unknowingly embraced a new identity: *"The identity of a sale closer"*. Now, when I look back, I am pleasantly surprised with what happened during that time. Due to this new identity which I had chosen, I could get resourceful, pick up a phone, improve my tonality, improve my skills and do roleplays with like-minded sale closers who were better than me. My new identity pushed me to take persistent action, and as a result, I got better and better. Despite starting out as a nerd with bad communication skills and no idea of what closing was, I became one of the best closers on the market.

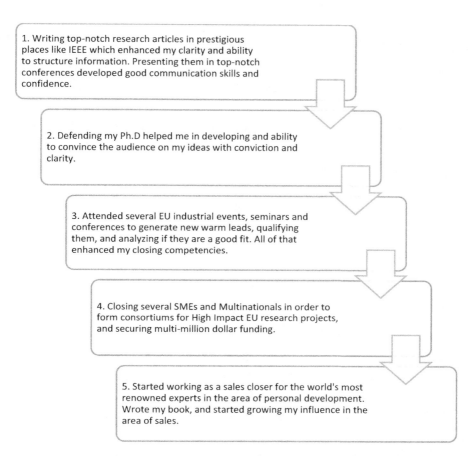

1. Writing top-notch research articles in prestigious places like IEEE which enhanced my clarity and ability to structure information. Presenting them in top-notch conferences developed good communication skills and confidence.

2. Defending my Ph.D helped me in developing and ability to convince the audience on my ideas with conviction and clarity.

3. Attended several EU industrial events, seminars and conferences to generate new warm leads, qualifying them, and analyzing if they are a good fit. All of that enhanced my closing competencies.

4. Closing several SMEs and Multinationals in order to form consortiums for High Impact EU research projects, and securing multi-million dollar funding.

5. Started working as a sales closer for the world's most renowned experts in the area of personal development. Wrote my book, and started growing my influence in the area of sales.

FIGURE 4: CHRONOLOGICAL DESCRIPTION OF DIFFERENT MILESTONES WHICH WERE ACHIEVED AS RESULT OF MY GROWING COMPETENCIES AS A CLOSER

I'll now describe what it takes to become a top-notch salesperson and the importance of closing as a transferable skill.

Sale Closing as a transferable skill

Figure 4: chronological description of different milestones which were achieved as result of my growing competencies as a closer shows the milestones which I achieved during my career where my sharpening competencies as a sale closer played a vital role. As you can see in Figure 4: chronological description of different milestones which were achieved as result of my growing competencies as a closer, you can apply closing skills in various contexts, and they can help you achieve multiple goals ranging from closing investors on your idea or negotiating a good deal. Your closing skills can also help you publish your research in prestigious journals by convincing the reviewers about the importance of your novel results from various perspectives. Your closing skills will give you the ability to close the audience on your ideas and beliefs. That will give you recognition and visibility, which will position you as an authority and expert in your area.

Can you become a top-notch salesperson?

Believe me, I wish I had the information which I am presenting in this book years back when I started. It would have drastically reduced my learning curve and saved me a lot of time. I had to learn by trial and error, reading countless books, and spend over 10K of investment in my personal development. So, stay tuned as we dissect the art of closing by starting at the mindset, beliefs and identity. We' later describe the tools and techniques that have made me tens of thousands of dollars each month consistently.

Also, in Figure 4: chronological description of different milestones which were achieved as result of my growing competencies as a closer, the most point which I want to emphasize is that irrespective of your background, expertise and job title, you can evolve into a top-notch closer, just like me and many other top-notch closers. Even though currently I am working as a sale closer, but, while acquiring the closing skills, I have never been a part of the closing team and I was working as a scientist, but it did not impede my evolution into a sale closer. The reason was that "my identity which I choose" motivated me each day to learn and explore the area of sales closing.

Are you thinking that you can't do it?

The Answer is: Yes, you can do it in the same way as many of my friends, colleagues and students have done already. You just need to follow and apply the 6-Step process described in this book and you will start closing sales in your industry with confidence. I myself made a transition from a scientific career to a top-notch sale closer using the same steps but it took me many years since I had to learn from trial and error. Therefore, read the book, apply the information presented at each step and you will succeed.

Skills can give you some success, but the right mindset and identity can offer you outstanding success!

—Subayal

SECTION 4:

STEP 2: MINDSET AND IDENTITY

CHAPTER 11

The Power of Mindset and Identity

Have you ever seen a renowned tennis player, basketball player, public speaker or guitarist together with your friends and you all said "wow, he is so natural"? And sometimes, you say "he lacks natural talent." Well, the situation in sales is no different. We all are conditioned by the electronic, print and social media in such a way that we focus only on the "current state" of a person's skills. Meaning, their current skill level and not on the hardships, challenges, setbacks and adversity which they faced when they started. It is essential to understand that one's mindset is the most fundamental and vital factor when it comes to achieving greatness.

With the right mindset and money beliefs, you will start thinking about life as a learning process, a growth-centric experience and give yourself the permission to start while being imperfect instead of waiting to be perfect from the onset. The fact is that you will never be perfect, and there is always room for improvement. I genuinely believe that we could be living in a very different world if we had all of the innovations that never made it to the market just because the inventors thought that they were not perfect, and people might not like them. Self-doubt and fear have deprived humanity of more than anything else in the world. Therefore, one's mindset and beliefs are the most crucial foundation in mastering the art of high-ticket closing and will be covered in-depth in this section.

Furthermore, many people in sales advocate wrong and baseless ideas like "selling is a natural talent" or "some people will never be good at sales, and some will just excel with minimum effort." That, to me, is lightyears away from the truth. For many years while working as a scientist, I was mostly confined to a black keyboard and black screen, but in parallel, I was closing industrial consortiums for multi-million EUR projects. According to most people, the two conflicting stereotypes—a nerd and a salesperson—cannot co-exist in the same human being. They think that being a nerd is something natural and being a salesperson is natural too, and two different natural creatures of nature cannot mix to form a genetically mutated crazy cocktail. I was a living example of that cocktail, and I thought exactly the contrary. So, anyone can master sales closing as you have already read in the first section of the book.

One thing which I observed about the best sale closers is that they all learned and mastered the art of sales closing by remaining committed and consistent. I am confidently stating that by the end of the six sections, even with no sales background, you can start a solid sales closing career with confidence. To become a master of the craft, you have to be consistent, avoid distraction, not treat it as a hobby, and show commitment. We have described strategies in section 6 to help you maintain your focus. Having no experience in sales is way better since you don't have to unlearn the things which don't serve you. During the last 12 years, I have helped many people from various backgrounds and at different skill level to master sales closing. Here are some examples:

1. **Newbies with no sales background who developed this skill and started closing sales with confidence within a month. This book does precisely that, meaning what I taught them is presented in this book. I also started with no sales background, so I know the fears while can impede our progress.**

2. **I have seen introverts and nerds develop the confidence to master the mechanics of sales conversation and take control of the call. I will teach you exactly how I taught them.**

3. **I have seen people who had sales careers but were not able to excel, grow and become experts in closing sales. This book reveals what they lacked and will help you nurture these essential skills. I have made sure that you**

get all the knowledge in this book which I transferred them.

All these people overcame two big challenges, and these were: The transformation of mindset and embracing the identity for themselves. Wanting to become a top-notch sale closer and embracing another identity, for oneself for example "a musician" or "an engineer" will be equivalent to "sitting on the seat of one car and having the hands on the steering of another vehicle." This applies not only to sales but also to other professions. If you read the story of athletes like Tiger Woods, Kobe Bryant, Tom Brady and Usain Bolt, you will realise that they all had one thing in common and that is "the right mindset" and "identity which they close for themselves." The best actors, leaders, visionaries and industry experts reach the top because they chose an "identity for themselves" which matched the image of "what they aspired to become" long before it became a reality and they reach the top.

CHAPTER 12

Importance of Mindset

According to Tony Robbins (Tony Robbins, 2019), there are specific patterns that cause people to be fulfilled, happy, remain healthy, feel alive, remain vibrant, have passion in their life and do well financially.

Also, these patterns help them emotionally, psychologically, spiritually and in their relationships. On the other hand, there are patterns which make people frustrated, overwhelmed, depressed, sad, lonely and cause them to struggle financially. Also, it is very important to understand what people need and want. By doing so, you're going to be a better leader, mother, dad or friend. There's a better version of you which is forged when you understand what drives you. I define the mindset as follows:

> *"A mindset is a set of patterns formed around different areas of our lives, a recurring frame of mind which determines the way we interpret and respond to situations and circumstances."*
>
> *—Subayal*

Some people might excel in their fields without the right mindset, but it is much more difficult, tiring and energy draining. Therefore, to become a top-notch closer while having fulfilment, freedom and happiness, you must work on your mindset. Without the right mindset, you cannot have a balanced life and excel in your sales closing career at the same time. In the beginning, I was an average closer and would only focus on strategies and techniques. It was not until I met my mentors who stressed the need of mindset that I started to grow very fast in this area. They told me exactly what was wrong. Immediately afterwards, not only did my closing skills begin to improve, but also new doors of opportunities started to open. In a few short years, I became one of the most sought-after sale closers in the industry, working with the top experts in the personal development field. I still remember the day when one of my mentors told me over dinner while pointing the finger at his forehead, "Subayal, you need to work on that, work on your mindset. This is the one thing which is holding you back." That was a life-changing moment there and then! Here is the conclusion of our discussion:

> *"To become a top-notch sale closer, the most important thing is the 'money mindset,' since it helps in developing the resilience, conviction and acumen required for becoming the best in this industry."*
>
> *—Subayal*

During our discussion, he told me I have to "change my pattern of thoughts about money—" he meant the money mindset. "That is going to manifest itself as a volcanic force and bring you abundance in life." These words helped me obliterate every obstacle in my way as I transformed into a top-notch closer in the industry.

Therefore, as a closer, if you're always thinking about money and commissions, working hard for every sale, if you are worried, nervous or doubtful, you're not alone in this boat. I have been through that experience; it was not the best of feelings, but the good thing is that I overcame this situation by working on my mindset. To upgrade your money mindset, you first have to understand how it is created and later on how you can update it.

For most people, as we grow up, the wrong beliefs about money get induced into our subconscious mind. But the question is: From where do these beliefs come? The answer is that a majority of kids grow up in working-class, middle-class or low-income families where there are financial issues, where parents argue about money, where they are living pay check to pay check and where they can only afford a short vacation in a year. When the majority of kids are raised in such families, the experience implants wrong beliefs about money in their minds which look like this:

> *"Money is scarce, it is in short supply, it is something which you have to hold close to you, it is something which you shouldn't lose, and it is something to be closely guarded. It is something to be it to be stored in a bank account for 0.5 per cent or one per cent yearly interest, and the wealth can grow very slowly. Life is meant to be consistent where a fixed wage is earned each month."*

Also, when we work in a firm or for a government as a bureaucrat, it has its own consequences such as:

> *"Trading time for money makes us believe that a specific, consistent value is attached to our time which we get in the form of pay check each month on the same day. This turns into the belief that life is consistent and not growth centric. This stagnates our growth, which limits our potential as long as we don't realise it."*

Now let us look at the impact of the second most important place, a school:

"When kids go to a school, how does it shape their mindset? Firstly, they see teachers in the school living pay check to pay check who tell them that you need to have a formal education to get a job. Secondly, they never tell the students that wealth which they will create will be a reflection of how many lives they have impacted irrespective of their educational background. You can earn a Ph.D., form an innovative company and impact millions or maybe billions of lives in the same way as the founders of Google did. Two Ph.D. students came up with an idea, and you can see where Google is right now. Furthermore, people with little or no education have impacted millions of lives too. Therefore, irrespective of your educational background, the only thing what matters is: How many lives you have impacted?"

This discussion can be summarised as:

"Merely stacking up university degrees is not something which will make you rich, but the value which you bring to the table irrespective of your educational background can make you rich".

—Subayal

When most people grow up in families where, when the parents go to a grocery store, they pick grocery items from the cheap shelves, what does that do to the mind of kids? When a kid wants a specific toy and the parents say, "No, it is too expensive and you cannot have it," the parents are implicitly telling the kid, "There is a shortage of money in this world, and the world lacks abundance." However, in reality, wealth is everywhere, and there are (at the time of writing this book) over 8 billion people on this planet. Therefore, it is just a matter of bringing value to the marketplace, in exchange of which a person can make money.

> *Anyone in a marketplace can create value, and the extent to which you create value will determine your financial success!*
>
> *—Subayal*

Right now, I'm using the Chrome browser to watch a video on YouTube as I am mustering my thoughts. YouTube is, again, a company that is owned by Google. Look at the impact that such services are making. Of course, the technology used to implement these services was around, but these things were only created after someone envisioned them and saw their potential. It has been challenging for me to overcome that paycheck to paycheck mindset which was implicitly installed for me by the education systems of four countries: Pakistan, then Sweden, then Germany, and finally Finland. At this point, you must be wondering, what do we as closers bring to the marketplace, and what impact do we actually create?

> *We as sale closers help businesses and people overcome their challenges by enabling them to access and utilize the right products and services.*
>
> *—Subayal*

Therefore, abundance is not something which is installed in our minds as we grow up. Instead of that, scarcity is something which is installed in our minds. People who get the opportunity to transform their money mindset create enormous wealth like Steve

Jobs, Bill Gates, and many other entrepreneurs who impact the lives of people and set up systems which make them money while they sleep. They don't trade time for money and instead impact millions or billions of people via their services or products. These services or products impact lives around the globe 24/7 throughout the year. So, there is not a lack of money and there is abundance in this world. Now the question is, how can you update your mindset? Below are the key points can help us in upgrading our mindset.

i. **Invest in yourself, meaning, invest in your personal development and get access to the right knowledge and skills.**

ii. **Upgrade your peer group. Remember that in most cases, your income will be very close to people in your peer group. Also, you will likely develop habits like the people in your close circle.**

iii. **Take advice from people whose lives you want. When you take someone's advice, you accept their life. It means that if you don't want the life of your parents or close friends, don't take their advice.**

iv. **You can create enormous wealth as long as you are capable of creating value for a big market.**

v. **Become growth-centric and keep on working on your mindset, skills, and don't trade time for money.**

In section 6, I have laid out a complete system which will make sure that you stay on track, move towards your goals and continuously improve.

CHAPTER 13

Importance of Identity

According to Tony Robbins (Tony Robbins, 2019), "One of the strongest needs within our personality is to make certain that our behaviour is consistent with our identity even if the identity we hold for ourselves is negative."

One critical point here is that "the identity which you choose for yourself" has the power to obliterate and overshadow the identity with which society, people or an organization labels us. The identity which you choose for yourself is the real deciding factor in the way you perform and at which level you play.

The reason for that is: When you choose an identity for yourself, it permeates into your habits and reflects into the way you operate. It is easier for us to install beliefs which are congruent with our identity, irrespective of the identity with which the society labels us. What is meant by that? The answer is that: There's a massive difference between feeling stupid, and knowing you are dumb. It makes an enormous difference in how we live our lives. We all feel stupid at times, but if we make the shift from feeling stupid in a moment to believing we are stupid, that belief about ourselves will overshadow all our behaviours for the rest of our lives.

Our identity defines us and creates the boundaries within which we live our lives. In other words, it is like the difference between being a person who has procrastinated in a moment and knowing one is a procrastinator. Once you decide that's who you are and you embrace that identity, your behaviours will become consistent with it, just because you need to be compatible with your own identity.

Therefore, you should be very careful about the labels which you create for yourself because they begin to define you. Also, you start embracing beliefs and behaviours which match your identity, and it also decides what you are willing to try and what you're not ready to try.

During my career, when I was still working as a researcher, the identity assigned to me by my organization was "research scientist," but I was still closing industrial partners for multi-million EUR EU projects. The reason was that I was a closer inside, and this was the identity which I chose for myself. This identity motivated me to learn more about closing, sales, and international business. As a result, I applied to one of the best business schools in Scandinavia, which had an over 95% rejection rate. Before I applied, the year before, the same business school selected about 20 students from over 700 applications. I told my colleagues about my desire to apply there, and they said, "What the hell! You are about to complete your Ph.D. in computer science, and you have no chance! This business school will never even look at your application."

But I had a different strategy. Remember that when you embrace an identity, the world opens up, and your mind starts craving ideas which will make things happen that will help you become a person who has fully embraced that identity. As a result, you will start looking for opportunities which will take you to your destiny.

I developed a plan which will take me to that business school. So, after thinking for a week, I got a great idea. I found that I was in fact enrolled in two universities as a PhD student—one in the city of Tampere and one in the town of Oulu. I once worked in Oulu in the area of wireless communications in Oulu university, and I was currently working in the same city with my current employer. Even though I later enrolled in Tampere University of Technology "TUT" which was in another town called "Tampere" as a PhD student. I was doing research in the area of Computer Systems and I was about to graduate.

The reason was that when I was working with my previous employer in Oulu, which was a research centre operating in Oulu University, they enrolled me to the PhD program in Oulu university and I did not cancel my enrolment. The university was close to my

72

office, so the next day, I went to student office at Oulu university and asked them for permission to enrol me in the advanced business courses which were offered by the business department at master level. The business school of Oulu university was not as good at that time. I knew that studying business courses there and getting excellent grades will help me transfer the coursework credits to the University of Vaasa, where I wanted to enrol in the Master program in international business. I knew that it was possible to transfer ECTS study credits to another university inside Europe.

They gave me permission to take business courses at graduate level so that I could use the credits as part of my course work for my PhD degree. I knew that if I got excellent grades in these courses, I could mention them in my CV and attach the transcript for the qualification process. Also, I asked my boss in the organization where I worked, and he made me an excellent reference letter stating that I had closed industrial consortiums for EU projects. Furthermore, I got references from two other business executives who were working with firms in the city of Oulu. I met them during a socializing event organized by the Business incubator in Oulu (Finland) during the time when I was taking business courses in Oulu University.

Now I had all the fuel to "close" the University of Vaasa on the idea that enrolling me will give them exposure and also diversification. I pitched the idea that I was a scientist from the best research centre in Scandinavia who wants to create radical innovations on the basis of the business experience (closing EU project partners), research experience (ICT area) and knowledge gained via advanced course in International business at Oulu University which I passed with excellent grades. I applied to the program after compiling my motivation letter mentioning all the aforementioned merits.

Over a cup of coffee in the morning, I told my colleagues that I was applying. They said, "Well, you are defending your Ph.D. thesis this year and you are a researcher. Some of us could not get a place there even though we had a bachelor's degree in business and we also worked in a few companies before applying. We had to complete our master's degree from another university." I said, "Well, let's see." And one month before defending my PhD degree, the big news came. I was selected, and I was thrilled. Not only that but I also successfully transferred the credits which I completed at Oulu University to University of Vaasa. So, not only would I get a prestigious business degree but also get it in almost half the time. My colleagues couldn't believe it, but once I showed them the letter of acceptance, they all congratulated me on my achievement.

So, you saw that my designation in my organization did not matter. I was closing partners for industrial consortiums; I closed the selection committee of the best business school in Finland and was super motivated to start my career in international business as a sale closer. The different milestones which I achieved throughout the different stages of my career are mentioned in Table 1, below. I have also mentioned the identity "which I chose for myself", the identity "assigned to me by my employer and society," and the outcomes during each stage of my career in Table 1.

TABLE 1: THE DIFFERENT STAGES OF MY CAREER, IDENTITIES (BOTH ASSIGNED BY EMPLOYER AND CHOSEN BY MYSELF) DURING EACH STAGE AND THE RESULTING OUTCOMES DURING EACH STAGE.

Stage of my career	"Identity assigned by employer and society" OR "Identity given by others"	Identity I chose for myself, OR "My identity"	Outcomes	Congruence with which identity?
During the Bachelor of electrical engineering 1999-2002	Student	Best VLSI designer and algorithm developer	Gold medal for Best Final Year project.	"My identity" OR "Identity given by others"
Master of Electrical Engineering 2005-2007	Student	Best VLSI designer and algorithm developer	94% marks and did Master thesis at the best research institute in Germany. The work was published.	"My identity"
2008-2011	Research Scientist	Research Scientist who stepped up his expertise to advanced distributed systems.	PhD in shortest time in 70 years history of my organization. Published over 12 research articles. We got an award from EU project in which I was involved. My organization awarded me with a prize.	"My identity"
2012-2018	Research Scientist	Sale closer	Closed the industrial consortiums. Closed the selection committee for the master's degree program in best university in Finland.	"My identity"

			Got the best grades in the courses completed in the program.	
November 2018-Now (Nov 2019)	Sale closer	Sale closer	- Left my research scientist job even though I was writing successful projects proposals. But my scientific job was just not fulfilling, and I did not want to do scientific work at all. -Lost interest completely in science. -Closed Mr. Peter Sage to work with him as a closer. -Got the opportunity to work closely with Mr. Pa Joof and create global impact by closing multi-million EUR projects.	"My identity"

Here are the conclusions which can be drawn from the information shown in Table 1.

i.   **The outcome (results which I got) at different stages of my career are in perfect alignment with the identity which I had chosen for myself during that time, irrespective of the identity with which society labelled me.**

ii.   **The identity which you choose for yourself is not something static and can change and evolve with time. So, you can shift your identity and replace the one which is not serving you with one that will help you in the future.**

iii.   Also, the identity "which we choose for ourselves" tends to overshadow the identity assigned to us by society.

iv.   Possibilities appear in life, which converge our personalities to our identity since our behaviour and actions are in alignment with our identity.

v.   We start to crave for the skills, environment and resources that will help us in getting closer to the ideal avatar, embracing the identity which we have chosen for ourselves. Hence, we get creative and start finding new possibilities which will convert us to that avatar.

Therefore, you must embrace the identity of a closer if you want to operate as a closer:

> *If you haven't embraced the identity of a closer, you will always be an average closer with merely moments of good performance. You won't operate as a top-notch closer because this is not who you are. You are not a closer!*
>
> *—Subayal*

When you make that shift and embrace the identity of a closer, your mental dialogue will go from this:

i.   Selling is something which irritates me, and it is something which I don't enjoy.

ii.   Closing was not my first career choice, so let us stay here for now and I will find something interesting later.

iii.   The roleplays are boring and a waste of time.

iv.   The questions which I ask don't help me in understanding the customer's problems and current state. I get many objections.

v.   The services which I sell are not worth the money we charge, and I will never pay that much for them myself.

vi.   Sales is not my favourite area, so I might shift my career at some point.

To this:

I.   I always find the time for role plays since they are interesting.

II.   I always try to dig deep into recorded roleplays to find areas of improvement, and I try to improve them during roleplays

III.   Closing is everywhere and working as a closer is fantastic since it helps me grow as a businessperson too.

IV.   I always try to find the best closers to do role plays with so that I can learn a lot in short time.

V.   I try to find the right environment full of elite closers to learn from, and I crave for more closing calls.

VI.   I have a hunger which helps me in improving each day as a closer.

Therefore, when you embrace the identity of a closer, you will try to search each day to find the best business partners to work with. Also, since you have embraced the identity of a closer and upgraded your money mindset, you will:

i.   Wake up each day with an iron determination, positivity and abundance.

ii. Effortlessly close more sales since you operate as a closer.

iii. Try to look at your mistakes as areas of improvements and learn the ways to improve these areas in future.

iv. Be able to close more sales and as a result, impact more people. At the same time, you will get fulfilment and happiness.

Therefore, upgrading your money mindset and embracing the identity of a sale closer will bring phenomenal results. You will be living like an elite closer each day, and you will transform yourself from a scared and cynical person to someone who radiates the confidence and positivity of a winner.

The more you contradict the avatar of a stereotypical salesperson, the more successful you will be as a closer!

—Subayal

SECTION 5:

STEP 3: UNCONVENTIONAL WISDOM

CHAPTER 14

The Contrarian

Real motivation underpinning a purchasing decision

It will help if you keep in mind that the extent to which a prospect "needs" the product or service is not the main factor behind a purchasing decision. The ability to buy is also not the factor which underpins a purchasing decision. If they want it badly enough, they will get resourceful and find money to afford it. That is why people go to a bank and mortgage a house, since they "want to" be the owners of a home in future and don't "want to" pay rent each month which will go to the landlord. They want to cover a small portion of the price of house each month which they will own one day, so they get resourceful and arrange funds via a mortgage.

Remember that it is a "want," so the need here is to have a roof over one's head which they will have in either case. No one can guarantee how long they are going to live or how long they are going to sustain their income levels which will ensure the mortgage payments. But a want, a desire, and a feeling of owning their own house is something which drives someone to mortgage a house. They know that that the ownership of a home will bring a sense of fulfilment in future and monthly mortgage payments are contributing to that ultimate goal or vision of owning their house.

Therefore, remember that the mortgage is a ticket for experiencing a life where they are home owners, are no longer paying rent, and can get that feeling of ownership which they craved for all the time during which they paid the mortgage. For 30 or so years, many other investment vehicles could have given them a higher return on investment, but no, they have a belief and a conviction that a mortgage is worth it because the associated feeling of satisfaction and fulfilment are worth taking that route. If making money was the only goal, they could have learned the way one can find motivated sellers who are old or going through a tight financial situation, buy a property near a city centre in the UK for 20% to 30% cheap and rent it out after converting it into an HMO (house under multiple occupancy). That will give them a whopping ROI of over 15-20% per year. But no, they go for the option which will provide them with more satisfaction today, because one day they will feel awesome by owning their own house. So, human psychology is at play in the background. We humans always buy with feelings and justify with logic.

Therefore, when a prospect is on the phone with you, you should not be convincing yourself whether the service or product you are selling is worth the price. It definitely is worth the price "with a high probability" to "the prospect" because they are on the phone with you for a reason. The same reason, as explained before, meaning they have an "emotional craving" or "a want" that will make them feel a certain way when they own it. Or else, the service or product will act as a vehicle and facilitate them in reaching an emotional state which they so badly crave for "right now".

Therefore, a gap exists which is filled by your service or product, and that is why they are on the phone with you. So, get any doubt out of your mind that makes you believe that your service or product is not worth its price tag. It might not be worth its price for you, and that is perfectly fine since you crave for many things which other people don't. So, a particular product or service is worth its price to some people, and you might not be among them. The business which sells that product or services is still in business because there is a demand for it and some people crave it.

Even if you think that a product or service is not worth its price, so what? Your opinion does not matter since you are not buying it. Your job as a closer is not to buy each product or service you sell but to help people realise their dreams, allow them to make their dreams a reality and help them own the product or services they crave.

So, it might not be the product or service that you desire, but it is not about you, it is about them. You are not selling to yourself; you are selling it to the person on the phone who wants it, and that is what matters. With this conviction, you will remove the need to "validate" your false idea that if something is not worth a specific price to you, the other person has to have the same opinion. Therefore, your perception of value might contradict with that of the prospect, and that is perfectly fine. Hence, you first must remove this mental block which you currently have before you start closing the sales of high-end products or services.

Selling high-end services and products makes sense.

As you always hear on media, in most professions, the rise in salaries is very shallow and it cannot keep up with the rising prices of different amenities of life. It is becoming more and more difficult to send kids to good schools, retire with enough money to live without worry, and have the mortgage paid in time before retirement. Therefore, wage earners are feeling stressed since they are not able to maintain the good living standards they once enjoyed a few decades back.

Hence, most of the middle class is living paycheck to paycheck and barely making ends meet. Therefore, you have the option to either move to the high-income level by equipping yourself with the right knowledge, strategies, and mindset, or else choose the other option where most likely you won't have a prosperous future. Globalization (due to which most manufacturing jobs are moving abroad), inflation (devaluation of currency due to printing of money by the central banks) and the influx of technologies such as internet of things and robotics into various industries are working against middle class wage earners across many industries. These realities will wipe out many jobs or will replace them with machines which will do them in a more reliable, consistent or efficient way.

Selling low-end products requires many units to be sold to make good profits. Therefore, the transaction size matters. You only have 24 hours in a day, and if are closing a low-end product or service over the phone which costs a few hundred USDs, even at a 30% commission and 50% closing rate, you won't be able to make even a McDonald's salary per month. Can you pay your bills with that? Do you want to live in poverty? Is that the future which you want to give you kids? Of course not. This example might be an exaggeration, but do you understand what I mean?

> *For a sale closer, selling low-end products or services is a license to financial nightmare, while selling high-end products or services is a license to prosperity.*
>
> *—Subayal*

Therefore, by selling high-end products or services, you can leverage your time better as a closer and make much more money at the same time. This will help you leave the middle-class income group faster and enable you to make diversified investments, which will keep on paying you each month in the form of dividends or rents. These multiple streams of income will not only increase in number as you find different opportunities to invest, but each one of them will also widen and pay you more with time. This exponential growth will not only help you retire in a much better financial situation but also much earlier if you want. Most of the firms selling their service to the middle-class income groups have gone bankrupt already. Do you want to be in a boat which is destined to sink? Obviously not, so leave that boat as soon as possible.

The second fundamental argument for selling high-end services is that such products and services mostly bring a lot of value to their target market in the form of an innovation, a unique user experience, a technological breakthrough or a brilliant personal transformation. Therefore, the product or service which you are selling will have a profound positive impact on the lives of people or else it will help them to get rid of bad habits. Meaning, these high-end services are of immense value, and as a result they act as a magnet for the people who are willing to pay a premium for them. Why on earth would you not sell a product or service at a price point which the market is willing to pay? Let the market justify the value of product or service which you are selling and let the perception of market work in your favour.

If the aforementioned points make sense, then why do you think that no one is going to pay for your product or service? Isn't the business owner still in business who is offering that product or service? Aren't people still buying it? In short, you should never think that the high-end product or service which you are selling is not worth its price.

Hence, you must keep in mind that selling valuable products and services at a price which the target market justifies by perceiving them as valuable is a good thing. A free market always dictates the value attached to the product or service, so you should let the market think about it and you should focus on your job of "sale closing". Also, since the value was created via blood sweat and tears, risk, years of trial and error, countless sleepless nights, lots of frustration, experts who persevered for decades, tremendous cost in terms of time, resources and money, therefore it is perfectly fine to ask for a price which will justify that and which the market pays with its own free will.

Positive perception and experience cascade!

Have you ever noticed that you and people around you always perceive higher-priced items as better, and that is why before they purchase them, they expect them to be good? Have you noticed that this is the same reason why so many people believe that

Ferrari is a fantastic car? Since Ferrari costs a fortune and the media advertises it as a great car, how can it not be? Even though people know that it breaks quite often, and you cannot drive it and enjoy the speed thrills on UK's motorway, and is not practical for many purposes, including taking a family of three somewhere. It loses its value at supersonic speed and so on. But it has to be good. As another example, Louis Vuitton bags are perceived as awesome because they are perceived like that by many people. Few people can afford it and media projects them in this way. Hence, how can the Louis Vuitton bags be ever cheap? It has been like this for their entire existence. Therefore, the point is that "whatever is expensive" is perceived as "valuable" by the masses. Also, you must have noticed that when people see something as valuable, they think it is worth taking care of, it is worth keeping in a safe place, it is worth showing off, and it is worth bragging about its goods and not flaws, because how can it be bad? Because it costs so much, and the common opinion of people is that it is so good. This is all psychological, and this is the way people behave.

The aforementioned points were confirmed when I came to know about a fantastic coach who offered her great coaching programs for a few hundred USD. As a result, very few people showed up to the live coaching sessions, even fewer got assignments done, and over 70% would leave the course midway. As a result, their lives won't change, their wellbeing will not improve, and also, they will focus only on the shortcomings of the program. They will go the extra mile to find all the minute shortcomings and overamplify them because the program was a few hundred dollars. In their minds, this is what was going on: How could that program be any good? How could that program be something worth committing? How can this program bring any value to their lives since the program itself is worth a few hundred dollars? It has to be substandard, bad, and cannot be worth their time. It cannot be something which they should take seriously and commit to. If something is worth a cheap holiday, how can it have a profound impact on the rest of their lives? The coach was barely making ends meet. So, just before going broke, she realised that she could increase the price, rebrand it, make the website a bit better and market it to a higher segment of the market. As a result, in the first batch, she got several students who gave fantastic feedback due to their commitment to the program. This created good social proof for her landing pages. That created a snowball effect, and since then, she has increased the price twice, and people want her service and willing to pay for it. But the value proposition, of course, was almost the same; over 80% of the course and website content had remained the same, but the price increased more than tenfold due to high demand and the love which it got from the students. Did you understand the hidden message in the examples above? The hidden message is:

> *The positive customer experience is mostly a realisation of the positive expectations!*
>
> *—Subayal*

Before purchasing the product or service, the customers develop positive perceptions from the opinions of people and their own brand perceptions. This shifts the focus of customer towards better features and positive experiences. As result, when the product is purchased, more emotional energy is directed toward the positive features and less toward the negative features. As a result, the positive features easily get attention and are remembered more. Therefore, the positive expectations developed before the purchase act as a filter for positive experience and features in the post purchase phase as shown in Figure 6.

Whenever a positive feature or experience is encountered, it leads to an interesting phenomenon called "confirmation bias," which stems from the fact that we humans always try to validate what we believe. Once we have validated the positive features, they further trigger another psychological response which is called hindsight bias. Due to this, the customers think that they knew it beforehand that this positive experience or feature would occur. They are convinced that the current outcome was exactly congruent with what they predicted before the purchase of the product or service. That develops a conviction which increase the focus on positive features as they use or experience them, instead of any negative ones in the service or product as shown in Figure 6. Hindsight bias is defined as:

> *"Hindsight bias is a psychological phenomenon in which individuals tend to overestimate their own ability to have predicted an outcome that they would have been unable to predict before an event took place." (Investopedia, 2019)*

Due to this, the positive features of the products or service are amplified as we use the product during its lifetime, and the negative features are suppressed. That is why the way they perceive the experience keeps on getting better. It has to be better because their emotional energy was consumed during their experience. It gets more and more difficult for them to shift their emotional energy and validate the negative features because this is not what they are aiming at or motivated to validate.

> ***The hindsight bias keeps consolidating the focus on the positive outcomes and away from negative outcomes during the lifetime of the product or service.***
>
> ***—Subayal Khan***

Furthermore, once the customers have purchased the product, the experience reflects in the conversations they have about the product or service to their friends and family online and in person. They are more likely to talk about the positive outcomes and experiences which they had while using the product or service. This implicitly enhances brand perception, when we hear about a particular product or service from the people we trust. Also, we are more likely to believe them and base our purchasing decisions on their opinion. Over time, it can snowball into a general perception of masses about the brand as more and more people share their positive experiences about the products or services.

The opposite is also true. Hence, inexpensive things are perceived as having "less value" and inferior quality. Therefore, they are loved less by people, which leads to negative or average expectations before they purchase the product or service. These negative perceptions shift the focus of clients towards the inferior features or shortcomings of the product or service. Hence, after purchases, whenever defects or inferior features are encountered, they are overly amplified since more emotional energy is directed to them. On the contrary, when the superior features of the service or product are encountered, they are suppressed, since less emotional energy goes to them. This phenomenon increases the probability of an average or bad end-user experience. Therefore, it is clear from this discussion that higher-priced products or services are not only more viable in terms of cash flow but also in terms of increased probability of better end-user experience. The increased cash flow further enables the service provider or product manufacturer to enhance the quality over time, and it therefore creates long term sustainability. On the other hand, lower prices cause price wars and suppress quality over time, which erodes the market share and act as a ticket to bankruptcy. The role played by higher and lower price points in the customer experience, enhancement of brand perception, and influencing the purchasing decision is shown in Figure 5 and Figure 6.

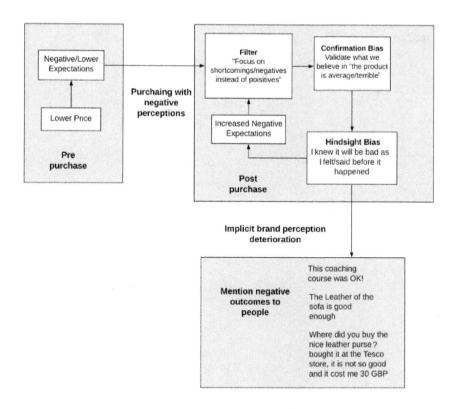

FIGURE 5: THE ROLE PLAYED BY LOWER PRICE POINTS IN THE CUSTOMER
EXPERIENCE, BRAND PERCEPTION ENHANCEMENT AND INFLUENCING THE
PURCHASING DECISION.

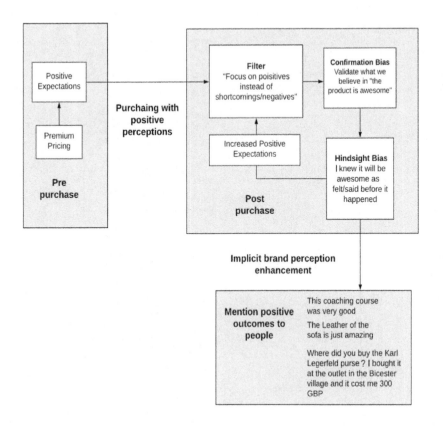

Detachment

The more detached you are from the features and benefits of the product or service during a closing conversation, the more energy of yours will be directed towards diagnosing the problems of the prospect. As a result, the prospect will feel more understood. Your ability to ask the right questions at the right time, just like a medical doctor, is what will take you to the core of the problem which your prospect is facing. The power of putting prospects first, not thinking about the commission, and focusing on their problems will help you gain their trust and create an environment where the prospect feels safe. When that happens, you will get the prospects emotionally involved, and this is what closes the sale. Therefore, you must understand the following essential points:

i.   **If you are attached to product features and benefits, it will project, the prospects will not get emotionally involved, and you won't be able to close the sale.**

ii.   **The more you understand their problems and the impact of the problem on their business, finances, health and emotions, the more they will get emotionally involved.**

iii.   **Your detachment from the product or service features and benefits gets them emotionally involved since they feel emotionally connected. Your emotional energy will be more focused on serving them, and this will project.**

When prospects feel safe, trusted, and see that your motivation is to investigate and understand their challenges, they will believe you more and they will get more and more emotionally involved. In this scenario, you are just trying to help them and not trying to shove the features down their throat, which pushes them away. Since most people try to avoid stereotypical salespeople, if you will act like one, they will try to avoid you too, and won't listen to you. The more you try to understand them, the more eager they will be to tell you more about their problems. This creates an environment which will motivate them to do business with you, and it also creates an excellent first impression.

Diagnostic Skills

Diagnostic skills encompass the ability of a closer to understand the problems and desired future states of prospects. As you get better at closing, you will start to automatically guess the challenges and desires of the prospect during a sales conversation.

In closing, the first step is to help prospects realise their current challenges as well as the impact which these challenges are having on them or their business. Once you help them understand this, you will also get a good understanding of their challenges during this process. That is the very reason why they are on the phone with you in the first place. So, the discovery of issues which a prospect has and the impact which these problems are having on their lives is the most crucial aim of a sales closing phone call. During this conversation, you have to identify the pains of customers, meaning the pains which these challenges have caused. The different levels of pains are described later in section 4. Your job is to bring these pains to the forefront. Many of those pains might be lying in the subconscious mind of the prospect. Uncovering these pains is an art, and this is what the pain discovery and diagnosis is all about. So, by asking questions, you will know what the current state of the prospect is, and the customers will also understand their problems well. Furthermore, your second goal is to help the prospects describe their desired future state by asking open ended questions as described in section 4. The more you practice and get better at it, the more successful you will be as a closer.

When you ask questions, you are actually (as the conversation goes on) trying to steer the conversation in a direction which will potentially reveal more pains of the prospects or reveal different aspects of their future state. In this way, you will be gathering more clues about the way their challenges and problems are impacting their lives, health and emotions. Also, you will be getting important insights about different aspects of their desired future state. As they talk more about their issues and desired future state, it gets them emotionally involved. Remember that the sale is always emotional and never logical. People make purchasing decisions based on emotions and justify them with logic.

Your main aim is first to understand their current state, which is comprised of their business, financial and emotional pains or challenges. Once you have done that, it is your job as a closer to help them paint a picture of the future state they want to reach once their problems are solved and pains are gone. After doing that, both you and prospect will understand the difference between their current state and the state where they want to be. This difference is called that gap which they must overcome. Only after identifying the gap should you describe the way your product or service will help them in bridging that gap. Therefore, as a closer, you help them see and understand how your product or service will help them in reaching the state which they desire and crave for so badly. The more you practice, the better your diagnostic skills will be. This is explained in detail in section 4.

Focus on their problems instead

Imagine a person who knocks at your door quite a few times before you open the door. As soon as you open the door, the person starts talking fast and a bit loud. That person is enthusiastic and desperate to tell you all the features of his product or service that he wants to sell you. You are irritated by the overly optimistic description of his offering, the way he talks, and the way he behaves. That person does not stop and drains himself out of energy. Even though he tells you tonnes of reasons why you should buy, you say "no" to him in the end. That is the reason why parents don't want their kids to become a salesperson.

Due to this, "selling" becomes such a non-favourite word for us as we grow up. That is why, whenever we think of a salesperson, not even a single positive thing comes to mind. All that is because a salesperson only focuses on "his service," "his sales pitch", "his opinions" and never bothers to ask about the problems which you are having. He never asked you how he could help you to overcome a business, personal, financial or any other problem that you are having. The focus is on himself and not you. He is self-centred, and that radiates from his words and body language. You pick up on that, and right after he leaves, you shut the door and feel very happy that he is gone. He did not listen to your problems and challenges and you feel so glad because you got rid of that irritating typical sales conversation. Most of us have that image of a salesperson in our minds, and it just never fades away.

Therefore, have you ever thought about an image of a typical salesman? I can bet that one thing which much have been in your imagination is a person who is chatty, pushy and very self-centred. His self-centred mindset persuades him to talk about the product or service that he is selling, and he cannot stop talking. Since a typical salesperson does not focus on the problem of prospects or gives very little energy to them, this results in the image of a person who is more focused on the business transaction and has little to no interest in what his or her prospect is going through.

When it comes to closing on the phone, many closers are still dancing to the tunes of a typical salesperson who knocks at the door. They are not focused on the problems which motivated the prospect to get in touch via a phone call or email and the impact which these problems have on their business, lives and finances.

As mentioned above, due to this, I have never seen any parent want their kids to be a salesman, since it reminds them of a person who knocks the door of their house where the moment the door opens a barrage of features are shoved down their throat. I am confident to state that:

Acting like a traditional salesperson has ruined countless sales careers.

—Subayal

That is why, in the sales conversation, you should talk as little as possible, while at the same time using questions to control the conversation. The less you talk, the more sales you will close.

Also, it would help if you asked questions that make them tell you why they should buy your product or service. The person who asks questions controls the conversation because when you ask a specific question, you steer the conversation in the direction of the topic about which you have asked the question. That is what the discovery process is all about, and in this way, you will be able to understand the problem of the prospect from various angles. At the same time, the prospect will also be pleasantly surprised to see that a salesperson is so caring and wants to help them instead of being pushy and acting like a radio station, broadcasting the features of a product or service.

> *Don't act like a traditional salesperson who sell via the same annoying pitch of features, benefits and so on. Instead focus on the problems of prospects and on serving them!*
>
> *—Subayal*

In this way, you will also be able to build a rapport with the prospect quickly. If you act like a typical salesperson, most likely, you will not be able to make a rapport, and you will project the energy and vibe of an ordinary salesman who has told the same features in the same manner to many prospects. Instead, you should listen to each prospect, build rapport and see what their needs are.

When you make them feel loved and cared, they will feel comfortable, safe and share their problems with you. In this way, you will be able to win their trust, and once you earn their trust, you will also get the sale closed. Remember that people buy people before they buy from them. You should always radiate your intent, and your intention should be to help the prospect. All the scenarios above create a situation where you contradict with every trait of a stereotypical salesperson and positions you as an expert. This is called pattern interrupt in the NLP (Neurolinguistic Programming, 2019) and is very powerful.

Team up, clarify vision, and close

It is imperative during a sales conversation to team up with the prospects and involve them in solving their own problem. Once you have identified the gap, know where they want to be in the future, and how their ideal life would look like, you ask them: "If our product helped you to solve your problems, how would that make you feel? What type of solutions you have tried before and did they work? What did you like and did not like about the previous products or services which you tried?"

> *Remember that you are skating over a frozen lake here, and you should not ask them: "How would an ideal solution to their problems look?" Or, "How can we precisely help you to mitigate the problem?" The reason is that if you do that, it will confuse them. They are on the phone with you because they don't know the solution. If they had known the solution, why would they be on the phone with you? So, team up with the prospects to get clarification on their problems and the impact which they are having on their lives, and remember that you are not on the phone to give them the solution or try to download the solution from the prospect's mind.*

Focusing on what they want (the solution) is the way to success in any sales situation, any industry, and any market.

—Subayal

Hence, during a sales conversation, you should always be focused on understanding what the prospects are looking for, what their pains are, and how can you solve their problems and "bridge the gap" via our services or products? In this way, you are putting the ball in the prospects court. You can ask them the results which they are expecting from an ideal product or service which will solve their problem. When they answer this question, you would tell them the way your product or services will help them achieve the results which they mentioned. Afterwards, you ask them, "Where should we go from here? Do you think it is the right fit for you?" And this is where the sale is closed. We will describe the concept of the gap and its layers in detail in step 4.

CHAPTER 15

Nonverbal Communication

Remember that your body language and tone are crucial pillars that will tremendously contribute to your success as a salesperson, since they bring an element of trust and credibility to your communicated message. They make it easier to get people emotionally involved and develop rapport. Body language and tonality are about "how you say it" rather than "what you say," and have a direct impact on the way your message is received.

You must remember that only about 7% of the effectiveness of your communication is a result of what you say. Surprisingly, this fact contradicts most books taught by sales gurus. It will help if you remember that the effectiveness of your communication mostly comes from your body language, which accounts for 55% of effectiveness, while about 38% comes from the tone of your voice. But as mentioned before, most business is now done over the internet. Therefore, most of the sales closing is done over the phone, and does not require a physical one-to one-meeting. Hence you don't need to work on your body language for this kind of sale closing, since closing on the phone only includes your voice. Therefore, tonality is the most critical factor in your phone closing career.

However, even though most purchasing decisions are now made over the phone without nonverbal inputs like your body language, there are some industries—like real estate and automotive—where most of the meetings with clients are face-to-face, in-person meetings. In these cases, body language plays a key role in the closing rates of sales meetings. Hence, you should focus on both aspects of nonverbal communication, i.e., body language and tonality, because they make a massive difference on the way "what you say" comes across to the other person. This chapter provides an overview of the importance and role of body language. We have dedicated the next two chapters to the two most important aspects of nonverbal communication which are body language and tonality.

Importance of Nonverbal Communication

As a salesperson, you must understand that we also have a parallel track of nonverbal communication which reveals a lot more information than our words, and sometimes disagrees with them. Therefore, the nonverbal communication cues that you observe will help you understand the way your prospect feels about your service or product. The gestures we make, the positions we place our bodies in, the expressions we wear on our faces, and the nonverbal qualities of our words all contribute to how others perceive us. Nonverbal communication creates a social language that in many ways is richer than our words.

Nonverbal ability plays an important role in understanding a person's warmth, reliability, and resilience. Although body language is not scientifically studied, in general, folded hands mean that you are closed to what someone tells you, but if you like what you hear, you are more likely to take an open stance. Moving your shoulders indicates a sense of disgust, frustration, or fear, while maintaining a large personal distance as you speak seems to be the social norm.

Role of Nonverbal communication

Nonverbal communication is one of the most important skills for a salesperson to have in order to understand the problems of the prospect. Nonverbal communication includes the way you listen, move, and respond in a sales conversation. When your nonverbal signals match the words you are saying, they build credibility, clarity and connection. When they are not, they can create tension, disbelief, and confusion. If you want to be a good communicator, it is important to be more sensitive to both the body language and the verbal cues of others as well as your own. Nonverbal communication plays five main roles:

Repetition: It repeats and strengthens your oral message.

Contradiction: It may be contrary to the message you are trying to convey in words. In this scenario, it indicates to your listener that you are not telling the truth.

Substitution: It can replace the verbal message. For example, your facial expressions convey a much clearer message than your words.

Complementing: It adds to your oral message or tone. For example, as a leader, if you pat your employees on the back in addition to giving them a bonus, it will enhance the effectiveness of your message.

Accenting: It underlines and emphasises the verbal message. For example, slapping the table reveals the importance of your message.

CHAPTER 16

Importance of Body Language

One of the keys to success in sales is your ability to communicate well through your nonverbal cues or body language, not just in the words you use. Body language is the informal communication of physical behaviour, gestures, and expressions. Whether you know it or not, you are constantly giving and receiving verbal signals when interacting with others. Your nonverbal behaviours, the gestures you perform, your posture, your tone and how much you communicate send strong messages. They can help you put people at ease, build trust, and draw others to you. At the same time, if used incorrectly, they can confuse people and reduce the effectiveness of what you are trying to convey. These messages don't stop when you stop talking. Even when you are quiet, you are still communicating.

It is important to know that when you say one thing, but your body language says something else, your listener may feel that you are not honest. When faced with such mixed signals, the listener must choose whether to trust your verbal or nonverbal message. Hence, your body language is in fact a natural and unconscious language that transmits your true feelings and intentions. Therefore, by improving how you understand and use nonverbal communication, you can express what you really want, connect better with others, and build stronger and more rewarding relationships.

Improving the Ability to Read Body Language

Here are the most important aspects of body language on which you must focus as a salesperson in order to enhance your ability to read the body language of prospects.

Facial expressions. The human face can express countless emotions. Facial expressions are universal, and we are familiar with the faces of happiness, sadness, anger, surprise, fear and disgust, which are similar across cultures.

Body movement and posture. This includes your posture, bearing, attitude and any subtle movements you make. It is important to understand the way your sitting position and walking or standing posture affects the way people perceive you.

Gesture. Gestures are strategies for your daily life. To get noticed when you argue or speak, you use your hands to wave, point, or call, often gesturing without thinking. The meaning of certain gestures can vary greatly across cultures. The hand-crafted "OK" mark gives a good message in English-speaking countries, but is considered offensive in countries such as Germany, Russia and Brazil. Therefore, you need to be careful while using gestures to avoid misinterpretation.

Eye contact. Visual senses are important to most people, and for this reason, eye contact is a key type of nonverbal communication. Eye contact is important in maintaining the flow of communication and measuring one's interest and responsiveness.

Touch We communicate a lot through touch. Think of a weak handshake, a warm embrace, a pat on the head, or other messages that allow you to communicate through touch.

Location Have you ever felt uncomfortable during a conversation because the other person was very close and in your space? We all need physical space, but that need varies and differs depending on the culture, the situation and the intimacy of the relationship between people. You can use physical space to communicate messages including intimacy, affection, aggression, or dominance.

Emotional Awareness

While enhancing your ability to read the body language of prospects, you can further improve your sales closing rate by improving your emotional intelligence. A salesperson needs to send accurate nonverbal cues to the prospect during a sales conversation or meeting. To achieve that, a salesperson needs to know about their own emotions first, along with the underlying reasons for their emotions and how they affect them. In this way, a salesperson can develop the ability to identify the signals sent by the prospects and the feelings behind these signals. This is where emotional awareness comes into play, which allows you to:

1. **Read other people's feelings and unspoken messages they don't send.**

2. **Build trust by sending informal signals that match their words.**

3. **Understand and respond in a way that shows others that you understand them and care.**

Many of us are disconnected from our emotions, especially the strong emotions such as anger, sadness, and fear. The reason is that we are taught to shut down or to not reveal our emotions. Even if your feelings are dismissed or frozen, you cannot eliminate them. They are still there beneath the surface, and they still affect your character. By enhancing your emotional awareness and dealing with unpleasant emotions, you will gain more control over how you think and act.

CHAPTER 17

The Power of Tonality

What is Tonality?

Tonality is an integral part of communication since it radiates someone's character via a non-visual medium. If you can use tonality in the right way, you can appear more valuable, build rapport faster, appear intelligent, and appear as an expert in your area; in this way, you will be able to influence others. The foundation of impactful communication is rooted in developing a rapport. According to Aldo Civico (Aldo Civico, 2019), who has worked in the area of conflict resolution for over 25 years,

"...Without rapport, there is no one interested in the message you want to communicate or the service you want to provide. Without rapport, there is little chance to influence or to persuade others."

Tonality acts as an emotional signal which frames the logical side of conversation and transcends the actual words that are spoken. This is very important since emotions, not logic, make the purchasing decisions. Also, the emotional cues register faster than the logical ones. The impact of tonality can be huge, as stated by Carl W. Buehner (Carl W. Buehner, 2019),

"They may forget what you said—but they will never forget how you made them feel."

Therefore, tonality is the most critical part of a sales conversation which must be mastered to get great results. It can invoke an emotional response in your prospects and enable you to connect with them emotionally, which is vital to make the sale happen.

Why is tonality so important?

Over the years, the most frustrating thing that I observed with the vast majority of salespeople is how many sales they are losing just because of the way they sound, or their "tonality." Meaning, their voice is the biggest obstacle in their success. As I mentioned at the beginning of the book, since more and more business is done over the phone, face to face meetings are becoming a thing of the past. I have talked to hundreds of closers, and they repeatedly complain that during their closing calls, they said something, but the prospect interpreted it in a very different way, heard something different or understood something different.

That makes them feel very bad, and it irritates them. The main problem is that the words which they say are all right but the way they say these words or the way they sound when they say them is where things go wrong. Remember that your tone is the most crucial pillar of your success and brings an element of trust of credibility to the communicated message. It makes it easier to get people emotionally involved and develop rapport. Tonality is about "how you say it" instead of "what you say," and has a direct impact on the way your message is received.

You must remember that only about 7% effectiveness of your communication is a result of what you say. Surprisingly, this fact contradicts the majority of books taught by sales gurus. It would help if you remembered that the effectiveness of your communication mostly comes from your body language, which accounts for 55% of it while about 38% comes from the tone of your voice. As mentioned before, nowadays, most business is done over the internet. Therefore, most of the sales closing is done over the phone and does not require a physical one to one meeting. Hence you don't need to work on your body language since closing on the phone only includes your voice. Therefore "tonality" is the most critical factor in your phone closing career.

In short, most of the purchasing decisions are made over the phone without non-verbal inputs like your body language, as is the case of the real faces to face meetings. Hence, you have to primarily focus on "the way you say it" because it makes a massive difference on the way "what you say" comes across to the other person.

One of the most essential things about tonality is that, when you're aware of your tonality, you can use it intentionally for creating specific effects in your sales closing conversations. It might sound counterintuitive to you in the beginning, especially when you are shy and nervous during sales conversations. However, with a little practice and feedback on your sales closing roleplays, you will see a big difference in the effectiveness of the message which you communicate across during sales closing conversations.

Hence, our tonality has the power to command attention as well as inspire your audience. But it also has the potential to make your audience fall asleep and bore it. With practice, you will be able to alter the way you pronounce and articulate phrases which will help you close more sales.

Different Aspects of Tonality

Tonality is comprised of distinct parts, each of which can be adjusted as per the situation to enhance the desired response. Remember that there is no such thing as a perfect tonality for a particular situation. Here are the main aspects of tonality.

Pitch

The pitch of voice shows: How low or high is your voice? Lower pitches are perceived as more masculine, while higher pitches are seen as more feminine. A "flat" pitch, which is called a "monotone," is the best and fastest way to lose rapport with someone, which means that they will disengage from the communication. Therefore, if you will not vary your pitch during a conversation, you will be perceived as "boring". You must have seen many teachers and speakers who talk like a monotone and help the audience in having a sweet relaxing short nap. The best speakers, teachers and politicians vary their pitch with inflexions depending on specific parts of a sentence. In this way, their voice invokes enthusiasm and interest as well as excitement about the topic.

Volume

Volume means: How your voice ranges on the scale of shy (quiet) to aggressive (loud). Just like pitch, if the volume of your voice is consistent, it won't be effective and will impact the rapport negatively.

If you're very quiet, some people will find it difficult to hear you and other people might speak over you, which will negatively impact your ability to assert yourself socially. A quiet voice is usually associated with intimacy, calmness, and security, but it lacks the power to invoke enthusiasm and command attention. On the flip side, people who are loud can appear as confrontational, arrogant or may even be perceived as crazy or volatile. So, even though you will get the attention, you won't be able to build trust with people and influence them. People are more driven and attracted to internal confidence instead of extroverted arrogance. Therefore, a variation of volume during conversation can be useful for conveying enthusiasm, ensuring calmness or commanding attention as you speak different phrases and words.

Pace

The speed at which you talk impacts how well people understand you and can enhance persuasiveness. It has been found in multiple studies that faster speech is positively associated with competence and extraversion. Moreover, the listeners rated the competence and social attractiveness higher for those people whose speaking speed was similar to their own. If you talk very fast, you will be hard and stressful to listen to, and you may also be perceived as agitated and nervous. As a result, people will not be able to process the words correctly, and it will be hard to build rapport and influence them.

On the other hand, speaking slowly means that your words will be readily understood but will irritate the audience since they will want more information faster. Just like the low pitch, speaking slowly will bore the listeners and they might disengage with you. Therefore, adjusting the pace during conversation will make it much easier to build rapport and trust, which is essential for the success of any closing call.

Articulation

Articulation is the way one physically moves the lips, tongue, jaw and teeth to create the sounds which will then contribute to sentences and words. Higher articulation makes it easier to communicate different views in complex conversations as well as convey basic desires and needs, which makes it easy to build rapport. Unclear speech can impact the closing discussions negatively, since prospects struggle to understand what you are saying which can lead to misinterpretation. If you master this aspect of tonality, there will be almost no ambiguity among you and the prospects. Furthermore, the use of filler words such as "um, ah, like" and "you know" will weaken your credibility. If you use these words frequently, the audience might perceive you as lacking knowledge, passion and not well prepared. In short, it reduces your credibility in influencing others and establishing rapport.

How to improve your tonality?

Improving your tonality is not challenging, and I will tell you exactly how I upgraded mine to the level that it is today. On the phone, you cannot use your visual cues or body language to reinforce the impact of your message. The only weapon in your arsenal is your voice. Hence, your professionalism, confidence, authority, expertise and friendliness must be radiated by your voice. As you practice the art of closing via roleplays and live calls, you must listen to the recording and ask yourself:

1. **Does my voice radiate confidence?**

2. **Does my voice radiate clarity?**

3. **Does my voice radiate certainty?**

4. **Does my voice radiate conviction?**

5. **Does my voice radiate assurance?**

6. **Does my voice radiate strength?**

7. **Does my voice reflect maturity?**

You can also ask for feedback on your roleplays from the closers with whom you do the roleplays. In this way, you can get an unbiased opinion and see things from a different angle. You can request a close relative or friend and ask them for their honest opinion. Also, you can try to find people who will give you honest feedback. You should listen to the feedback and criticism and take it as a "constructive criticism." This will improve your tonality and enhance your closing skills tremendously.

CHAPTER 18

The Power of Experience, Desire and Wants

While walking around in the "Bicester Village" in Oxfordshire UK, I found many people buying luxury goods of top designer brands. As they walk across the designer outlets, their eyes could not get enough of the displayed products like bags, jacket, suits and other luxury items. The whole experience of shopping in Bicester Village (Bicester Village, 2019), starting from the clean tiled streets, well-dressed salesmen, fragrant flowers planted everywhere, and nice seating converges to one sentence, in my opinion:

> *"Availability of premium products from different high-end brands in one beautiful place called Bicester Village which creates a perception of unmatched luxurious shopping experience."*
>
> *—Subayal*

And the main objective of Bicester village is to: *"Fulfil the desires of people such as feelings of significance and status which is done by providing them with an opportunity to buy the products which will deliver these feelings."*

Let us look at Rolex watches. The power of perception creates an experience of luxury, and as a result, the "Rolex watches" are perceived as the best watch a man can own. Therefore, the watch is more like a status symbol for the rich. In Table 2, we have compared the features and functionalities of Rolex to other watch brands to investigate the actual reason behind its brand perception and qualities which make it so much loved and wanted.

TABLE 2: COMPARING THE FEATURES OF ROLEX TO OTHER WATCH BRANDS TO INVESTIGATE THE EXACT REASON BEHIND ITS BRAND PERCEPTION.

Rolex features and attributes examined.	Does it lead the market? Yes/No	Comparison with other brands based on the same feature.
Most reliable.	NO	Breitling is more reliable and so is Omega.
Most features.	NO	Casio has way more features.
Most comfortable.	NO	It is cumbersome for many people.
Most high-tech.	NO	Casio and the Apple Watch are more high-tech.
Most innovative.	NO	Apple and many other brands are more innovative.
More robust.	NO	Breitling is more robust and reliable.
Most expensive materials.	NO	Many brands use similar materials but cost less.

From Table 2, it is evident that many other brands with much lower prices far exceed Rolex in terms of functionalities, technologies and features. But then, why people give it so much love and want to own it? Here are the precision reasons behind the brand perception of Rolex watches.

1. **Association: Great golfers, great tennis players and jockeys own it who are famous and wealthy. So, it creates a perception of association with the rich and famous.**

2. **Status:** Rolex has always been sponsors for Wimbledon and other famous tournaments, so it means that they share the prestige and status with these tournaments.

3. **Legacy:** Their ads show the history of Wimbledon and other famous sports tournaments in conjunction with Rolex. Hence it creates a perception of associated with the legacy of these tournaments. This association transcends many generations of sportsmen, which gives the brand its firm place in history, the current world and the future.

4. **Exclusivity:** On the best sportsmen own it, and you have to earn it.

Now you tell me, who wouldn't like to be in these shoes and own a watch which will help them live these moments without being a famous sports celebrity themselves? Therefore, it is about an emotional craving for the same feelings that famous sports celebrities have which will give us an uplift of mood. Therefore, people buy Rolex and other expensive products and services of high-end brands because they make them feel more important or because they think that other people will perceive them as richer, classier, of higher status or more professional.

Therefore, people buy experiences and perceptions and not products. Many times, you must have heard the phrase "people buy people before they buy something from them" and the reason is their brand, status, contribution to a field or image which they have due to their reputation or status. So, if a high-end brand has created a reputation like the personal brand of Tony Robbins, people will happily pay a premium for its products and services. Since Tony Robbins is a pioneer of the personal development industry, his reputation has created a "perception" due to which people love him. There might be many more knowledgeable people, professors, renowned psychologists and even better coaches, but he has a better reputation, and therefore more people want his services. So, when you ask yourself: "Why do you buy the services of Tony Robbins even though they cost so much?" You justify the price by telling yourself that it is worth the money. That is why the tickets for his events sell effortlessly. No doubt, his services are excellent, but you get the point. It is a simple and straightforward reality which is underpinned by one fact.

> **It is not** *"A Thing"* **but** *"The Thing"* **which people crave.**
>
> **—Subayal**

Therefore, people are more eager to base their purchasing decisions on the emotions and feelings which set a brand apart from others. Hence, remember that buying decisions are based on emotions, but they are always justified by logic. And it is also not so much about the value; it is more about the brand. So, for example, people care for expensive things not because valuable items will help them optimally achieve something or perform a function differently. The fact is that people love costly stuff because they give them a different experience which invokes and provides them with the emotions they crave.

So, let's pretend that a person buys a Ferrari and then another person buys a Lexus. When it comes to comfort and reliability, a Lexus is better or as good as a Ferrari. But the experience which you get by owning a Ferrari is terrific because of the looks that you get from other people, the attention it grabs and the way its engine sounds. However, if you look at the two cars from a logical lens, you will find that in the UK, you cannot drive Ferrari over the speed limit on roads. Lexus is more reliable, and within the speed limits, it provides more comfort, more space and more reliability. However, Ferrari makes people feel more important since it is a status symbol. You must keep one thing in mind.

People pay a premium price for experience and feelings and not for the functionality.

—Subayal

When it comes to purchasing a car, the main logical reason behind the car purchase is to go from one place to another conveniently, and that is why cars were invented in the first place. However, experience is a combination of feelings such as the feeling of significance, the sense of prestige, the feeling of status and the feelings invoked when people look at you. When you are driving it or when you go from one place to another in a Ferrari, you feel amazing.

Now, if we ask ourselves a question: What does a car do? Our answer will be: A car takes us from one place to another. So, the point is that both Toyota and Ferrari are cars, and they will help you achieve the same objective. Now, what separates Ferrari from a car for which people pay such a high price? The answer is that Ferrari is a car, and it is a type of car which helps you feel more significant, of higher status and wealthier, and these are the emotions which people crave. That is why people love to have a Ferrari. They love it because it is "the car" which gives them an extraordinary experience full of emotions which they want.

Therefore, as already mentioned, it is not about service; it is about "the service". It is not about a coach; it is about "the coach." That is why it is always important to keep in mind that people pay thousands of dollars for certain services, products, coaches and consultants because they have strong brands which create a particular perception about them in the minds of people. It leads to a straightforward conclusion, which is that people don't buy the products or services, but the emotional state which they want to reach as a result of owning or experiencing them.

In

Table 3 and Table 4, we are looking at two different markets and examining the way different brands are positioned in these markets as far as the price points are concerned. We want to investigate the reasons why people pay more for high-end products and less for low-end products in these two market segments. We want to identify or shortlist similar patterns in these very different market segments to draw meaningful conclusions. We have chosen the lady's bags in the accessories market and the SUVs market segment.

The main question which we are asking is:

What do the customers pay for?

In other words,

What are the deciding factors for the vast price differences between different alternative products in these market segments?

TABLE 3: COMPARING TED BAKER, CARL LAGERFELD AND LOUIS VUITTON BAGS IN LADIES BAG MARKET SEGMENT

Reason of paid Price	The products at different price range			Price paid
	Ted Baker Bag	Carl Lagerfeld Bag	Louis Vuitton Bag	
Utility centric price: Price paid for: Functionality, reliability and utility.	Same functionality (Handbags of similar size and can hold similar items)			**100-150** **GBP**
	Same reliability: Cow or Calf leather which can last many years			
	Same materials: Cow or Calf leather			
Emotion centric price: Price paid for: Uniqueness, Perception, Perceived craftsmanship, Status, Brand perception, Scarcity, Prestige and Other associated Emotions and feelings.	Moderate total price 130-200 GBP	High total price 300+ GBP	Very high price (1500+ USDs)	**0-1200+** **USDs**
	Lower *perceived* value in terms of craftsmanship, status, brand perception, and other emotion centric trails.	Higher *perceived* value in terms of craftsmanship, status, brand perception, and other emotion centric trails	One of the Highest *perceived* value in terms of craftsmanship, status, brand perception, and other emotion centric trails	

Reason of paid Price	The products at different price range		Price paid
	Toyota "Land Cruiser Invincible" 5-door automatic SUV £55,345 	Rolls Royce "Cullinan" 5-door automatic SUV £285,000 	
Utility centric price: Price paid for: Functionality, reliability and utility.	Same functionality: Takes you from one place to another, off-road and cross country		**55K GBP**
	Reliability: Toyota "Land Cruiser Invincible" is more reliable.		
	Efficiency: "Land Cruiser Invincible" is more efficient.		
Emotion centric price: Price paid for: Uniqueness, Perception, Perceived craftsmanship, Status, Brand perception, Scarcity, Prestige and Other associated Emotions and feelings.	Low total price £55,345	Very high total price £285,000	**0-230K GBP**
	Lower *perceived* value in terms of craftsmanship, status, brand perception, and other emotion centric trails	One of the Highest *perceived* value in terms of craftsmanship, status, brand perception, and other emotion centric trails	

119

We can see that the utility, reliability and functionality never motivate a buyer to pay a premium for a product or service. In other words, what truly motivates a buyer to pay premiums for a product or service which has same "functionality" and "utility as an alternative product or service can be its uniqueness, perceived craftsmanship, status, scarcity, prestige and other associated emotions.

Emotions execute the sale of a high-end product or services while logic justifies it. For low-end products and services, emotions have little to no involvement in the execution of a sale.

—Subayal

Hence, People buy high-end products and services to experience certain emotions which they crave. People pay higher prices for these products and services because they are offered by the world's famous luxury brands, leading industry experts and best coaches in the world. Your job as a sale closer is to help the people in possessing the high-end products or accessing the high-end services which they want and love.

CHAPTER 19

Projecting your Value and The Myth of Affordability

You must have seen several salespeople talking about the product or service in a way that is very irritating. They say things like:

"Who is going to buy this shit?"

"Who the hell on earth is going to pay this much for it?"

"I won't pay this much for that crap in my wildest dreams, and it is merely ridiculous. How can a person pay 1000 USD for a box of Cuban cigars when you can buy Marlboro for 20 times less the price? I wonder what goes through the minds of those people."

This attitude is just like taking an axe and chopping up one's sale career.

Remember, never project your value on the client. If the Louis Vuitton bag is not something you like, it means you don't value it. But it does not mean that your prospect will also not appreciate it and think in the same way as you do. If other people believed the same as us, we wouldn't have any arguments with our wives, girlfriends, parents, siblings or friends.

Did you ever have a discussion with your family members or friends about something where you are justifying that something is better, and your friend or family member disagrees with you and has the opposite opinion?

Of course, you must have had such discussions unless you are living in the basement of your parents' house or suffering from social anxiety, which I don't believe is the case. Such arguments drain us out of energy since you and the other person both try to justify your own perception of value.

That is why for some people, paying for expensive cigars is justified, because they value it. For other people, a cheap cigarette is what they like. So just because you don't appreciate a product or service enough and won't pay 2K, 20K or even 200K USDs for it, does not mean that someone else won't pay that much for it. The reason is that we attach value to certain aspects of a service or product, and those aspects define our perception of value. Others might attach value to other aspects of the product or service and thus their perception of value is different.

Hence, never look at things from your perspective. If you don't value something, it does not necessarily mean that someone else is also not going to appreciate it. Therefore, during a sale closing conversation, always have this belief and conviction because it will project. If you are insecure about the price of the service or product because you are biased to your judgement of value, you will project it, your tonality will radiate it, and you are most probably not going to make the sale because the prospect will absorb your own judgment. That is the reason why I always emphasize the eradication of this false belief that if you don't value something, the prospect on the phone also won't appreciate it either.

> *It is not your perception of value, but it is rather their perception of value which matters.*
>
> *—Subayal*

Furthermore, people afford what they want to afford and not what they can afford. If that were not the case, many people would not borrow a loan from a bank to mortgage the houses or flats where they live. In other words, if people won't mortgage their homes (which they cannot buy in cash), they would be living on rent. Likewise, no one would be buying cars for which they pay monthly instalments that they cannot buy in cash. See, the point is that if people want something badly enough, they will get resourceful and find the money. If your product or service can give people emotions and experiences that they crave, it will become an "object of desire" for them. It might not be an object of desire for you, but for them, it might be, and that is very important. It is not about logic, but about experience and emotions. If your product or service is something which the prospect loves and wants, they will find the money to buy it.

People afford what they want to afford. If they want it badly enough, they will buy

—Subayal

All the luxury brands are made with the user experience at the core. It is about the feelings of prestige that come with the product, the looks which they get when they own it, the way it makes them stand out, the way it helps them become a part of the trend which has gone viral on social media, or any other emotion or feeling that they crave. They want to get into a specific emotional state by purchasing a product or service, which is their object of desire. Therefore, high-end products or services are just vehicles to help people realise their dreams or reach a particular emotional state made up of feelings that they desire. So, we conclude that people pay a premium price for emotions, experience and feelings and not for utility, reliability, usability or functionality.

The pains of prospects reside at different levels. As a closer, you should be a master of uncovering these pains!

—Subayal

SECTION 6:

STEP4:
THE LAYERS OF
PAINS AND GAP

CHAPTER 20

Three Levels of Pain

Countless times in my career, I have seen salespersons who lost the sale because they were not able to overcome the most prominent mental obstacle which salespersons have: shifting the focus from themselves to the prospect. They don't realise that it is not them who are to be served, it is not them who are looking for a solution, it is not them who have an unsolved problem, it is not them who are ultimately going to decide whether the solution is a good fit or not.

Due to this, most salespersons even nowadays mainly talk about product features and competitors. They remain attached to their service or product and drain themselves out of all emotional energy to justify that they have the ideal product or service, which will help the prospect. The crazy part is that they assume that they have the best solution without even knowing and understanding the problem which the prospect is having.

That is very counter-intuitive yet very common. That is precisely the reason why many salespersons are not liked. Just think about it for a second: would you ever trust a doctor who recommended medicine without even talking to you about your health problem? I believe that you would feel very unsafe, and want to run out of his clinic as soon as possible. Though a doctor and salesperson are different labels assigned by society and two different professions, remember that we humans analyse both scenarios through the lens of emotions. In the same way that you wouldn't trust a doctor who behaved like a typical salesperson, you will definitely trust and feel safe in the presence of a salesperson who acts like a doctor with excellent diagnostic skills.

Therefore, you must shatter this image of a stereotypical salesman when you initiate the closing call with the prospect. That is called pattern interrupt in NLP (Neurolinguistic Programming, 2019), and once you do that, the prospects become comfortable, feel safe, feel loved and cared for. You start acting like a doctor who is there to diagnose a problem and recommend the right medicine.

So, as a salesperson, you must enhance your diagnostic skills to identify the pains which the prospect is experiencing to make them feel understood and get them emotionally involved.

I identified after countless sales calls that there are three levels of pains which the prospects experience. These are the surface level (or ego-level) pains, the financial pains and the emotional (or personal) pains. In my sales career, I identified these three levels of pains myself after a lot of frustration, trial and error, brainstorming, and learning about human psychology.

When a prospect gets on the phone call, they will first mention the different problems which are related to the current state of their business or lives which they want to overcome. I call them the surface level pains. These problems in their business can include sub-optimal business processes, design of new product features, increasing competition, a lack of talented workforce in a particular area, finding a supplier to take care of the rising costs of raw materials, the inefficiencies in the supply chains, the decreasing demand of their services, a way to raise a cheap loan for business, finding right IT consultants for digitalization of business process, streamlining the business processes as per changing regulations and finding renovation experts for their rental apartments portfolio. The surface-level problems can also be confined to a person himself, such as lack of leadership skills, disturbed sleep patterns or problems in their relationship with a spouse.

Now, you can see a pattern here. All these problems are business problems or surface problems related to the prospect's life. Once solved, they will make the business more strategically agile, the business processes more efficient or help their business survive and thrive. Also, once the surface level problems of a person's life are solved, it will make their sleep patterns better, improve their leadership skills, or improve the relationship with their spouse. These problems form the topmost level of the pain pyramid and are called surface level pains. To uncover the surface level pains, you ask open-ended questions which will get them talking about the problem that they are having.

Now, let us dissect the concept of financial pains. One thing which you can observe is that these surface-level pains have a financial cost attached to them. So, for example, for each of the aforementioned surface level pains, a financial consequence can result. The financial pains form the second level of the pain pyramid. In order to uncover the financial pains, you first ask (intermediary) questions which will reveal the underlying reasons as to why they think these problems are worth solving. Once they have answered them, you will get essential clues. Sometimes, they will even mention the financial impact straight away, and you don't need to ask the second set of questions to uncover the financial pains.

When you uncover the financial pains, you also cost the problem which will give you valuable hints for the final set of questions for discovering the emotional pains. At each stage, you must note down the key pieces of information on a paper as you listen with a sincere intent to help them solve their problem. Remember that it is about them and not you. Each column of Table 5 shows the questions asked for uncovering each level of pains and their answers in many sales scenarios. Each row represents a potential sales conversation where the answers to questions are mentioned. Therefore, each row represents the way pains were uncovered at each level as a result of the prospect's replies to the set of questions asked.

TABLE 5: UNCOVERING THE SURFACE-LEVEL AND THE FINANCIAL-LEVEL PAIN.

Surface Level Pains	Financial Pains	
Asked Questions: What motivated you to call me today? What are the main challenges which you are facing currently?	**Asked Questions (intermediary questions)** Why is it so important to you? How has it impacted your business?	**Asked Questions (last set of questions)** How much it has impacted your business financially over the past 3 months/six months or year? How much revenue do you think you have lost as a result of that?
Potential answers to questions: ↓	**Potential answers to questions:** ↓	**Potential answers to questions:** ↓
Product features need upgrading.	Because our products are losing customer interest, as a result we might lose 20% market share.	20% market share in UK where we currently operate will be well over 200K over the last three months alone.
The increasing competition is eroding our profits.	Because there are similar products sold on Amazon and people don't buy from our Ebay and Amazon stores that much.	We were selling well over 30K per month but now it has gradually gone down to 10K per month over the last 4 months.
The lack of talented workforce in the software development industry is affecting our business.	It is important because we cannot roll out next versions of our recruitment software for the clients so that we can keep up with changing value proposition of the competition.	If we did not hire the best software engineers, losing just 200 clients out of 500 will cost us well over a million USD over the next quarter.
We want to find a new supplier which can supply us at reasonable cost in the long run.	It is a nightmare since our current supplier, though reliable, just costs too much and it is time to switch. We will go bankrupt if we keep on having him as our supplier.	We found that we are paying 20% more than the market price and it can be around 8K USD each month for our family business.
We want to find a supplier to mitigate the	The shelf life of milk is reduced by one or two	We can honestly lose much of our business if something

129

inefficiencies in our dairy supply chain.	days since the delivery vehicles are never on time at the farms. We have heard enough excuses. Another problem is that they don't have any means to track the origin of the milk and if some bacteria of anything harmful gets mixed into the milk, we will be held responsible and our brand will get negative press. That will tear our brand to shreds which my father and mother created half a century back.	nasty happens. With a modest estimate, if we just lose our cheddar cheese business which brings in just 10% of our overall revenue, we are talking about 100K per quarter in losses. That can happen due to lawsuits by regulatory bodies. Due to lack of timely deliveries, we are already losing 30K each month for our overall business portfolio including cheese, yoghurt and flavored milk.
The decreasing demand of our services will take us to bankruptcy.	Many new software design firms are popping like mushrooms in India and they do work with reasonable quality. We think that the decreasing demand is going to take our multimillion-dollar revenue firm out of business if it goes on like that. If we had included complementary services like strategic industry analysis, competitor analysis and wire frame design in our services, we would have easily tackled this problem since we will get a competitive edge over the competition, but we don't have the right workforce and we need to hire them as soon as possible.	Not having the right workforce is already costing us over 120K EUR in revenue each month and it can easily double in next quarter. We simply cannot survive like that.
I want to know a way to raise a cheap loan for business so that it won't affect my bottom this much.	The 10% interest rate is ridiculous, and I went for it because I had a new firm registered. Instead of living with the regret for the rest of my life of not realizing the business idea, I decided to take a high interest loan. However,	It costs me over 3K EUR per month which is huge considering the size of my company which has just two business partners.

	now I realise that it costs too much to service that loan which is eroding my profits each month.	
We want to find the right IT consultants for the digitalization of our business process.	Our competitors have already replaced the manual customer service points with the digital ones where they swap cards and bar codes of grocery items which makes things more convenient for consumers. It is easier for the shoppers since they don't have to deal with the customer assistant at the payment terminals and they don't have to wait in the queue. As a result, no bottleneck is created. Due to this, the customers shop from nearby store. The customer survey reveals that we are better in every respect, but the long queues just push them to go to the other store.	The competing store which is just 100 meters away is simply cashing on the inefficiencies of our business process. It is costing us over 20K EUR in the form of net profits each month which is humongous.
My wife and I are finding renovation experts so that we can rent the apartments in our portfolio to better tenants or for a higher rent.	The tenants which we have currently in our ten apartments can happily pay 20% more rent if we renovate them. The problem is that renovation is not something which we have experience in. I talked to a few guys, but they were charging too much. We want to give this work to a company which will renovate all our ten apartments in the city center at a reasonable cost.	After renovations, we can easily generate additional yearly net profits of around 40K GBP from our portfolio of 10 apartments because the apartments are in a good location.

After uncovering the financial pain, you now have the fuel to transition into the impact on their emotional state. In this step, your tonality and rapport which you established so far will play a vital role. The first two levels of pain will give you essential hints and therefore facilitate the process of uncovering the personal pains.

The typical personal pains contain emotions like fear, anxiety, insecurity, lack of self-belief and lack of self-confidence. These pains can be uncovered by asking questions like:

1. **How has it impacted you emotionally?**

2. **How does that make you feel?**

3. **How has it impacted your life as an entrepreneur/professional?**

4. **How has it affected your well-being?**

5. **How has it impacted your relationship with your family members and friends?**

At this stage, the most critical point is to understand the current emotional state of the prospect since their emotional state is the most important motivating factor for them to be on call with you. Even though they never tell you about the emotional impact of the problem straight away in the beginning of the conversation, it is your job to uncover emotional pains or personal pains. After getting answers to these questions, you can ask follow-up questions to reveal more details and pains. For example: That must be painful, can you tell me a bit more about *"mention_the_uncovered_pain_here"*?

i. **How long have you been feeling this way, have you consulted someone else?**

ii. **How do your family members and relatives feel about it and how does that make you feel?**

iii. Has it also impacted your role as a husband or father?

iv. How important it is for you to remove that pain?

v. How much can it cost you if you don't solve this problem in the coming five years?

The aforementioned pains can be illustrated in the form of a pain pyramid which represents an iceberg. The most significant impact on the outcome of the sales conversation are the emotional pains which reside at the base of the iceberg, here shown as the pain pyramid. The surface level pains form the tip of the iceberg, which have the least impact on the outcome of the sales conversation. The real truth is that in most cases, the prospects will also not tell you the surface level pains in the beginning. You have to first ask questions for uncovering the level 1 and level 2 pains, and afterwards ask questions which will reveal the emotional pains. During this process, your aim will be to get the prospect emotionally involved via increased trust. In this way, they will tell you the impact of emotional pains on their lives and the effect which their problems can have on them in future if they are unable to find a solution.

It must be noted that in order to uncover the personal or level 3 pains, you must know and understand the emotional desires of the prospect by asking open-ended questions with good tonality. If you are thinking about the commission or if you are needy, you will project that. They will feel it and know it even if you want to conceal it with words. Your job as a closer is to use emotional intelligence and diagnostic skills with an intent to help and serve the prospects. When you do regular roleplays, and when you talk to more and more prospects, you will get better at it. When your intent is right, it will project, the prospects will feel it and trust you more and more as the sales conversation proceeds. They will start sharing the limiting beliefs, the fears, the anxieties, the insecurities and the childhood traumas which haunt them to this day. These are emotional or Level 3 pains and underpin the Level 1 or Level 2 pains.

They will readily tell you the level 1 and level 2 pains but will only share the level 3 pains with you once you direct your mental and emotional energy towards them and focusing on their problems. The prospect will sense that radiated energy which will motivate them to trust you. It will make them feel safe. Without that, they will not share their personal pains with you. You see, every logical and financial pain has an impact on our emotions and results in level 3 pains. If that was not the case, the prospect won't call you. Remember that they are on the call with you because they feel a certain way—even though at the beginning of the closing call, they will tell you the logical pains and in very few cases, the financial pains. The Level 1 and Level 2 pains and mostly confined to the conscious mind while the Level 3 pains are mostly confined to the subconscious mind. That is the very reason why uncovering the Level 3 pains requires a high level of trust, emotional intelligence and are not shared by the prospect at the beginning of a conversation. The aforementioned facts are summarized in Figure 7, while the pain pyramid is illustrated in Figure 8.

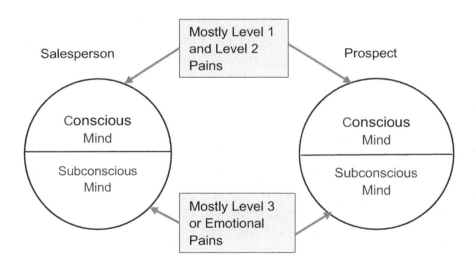

FIGURE 7: FIGURE SHOWING DIFFERENT TYPES OF PAINS RESIDING IN THE CAUTIOUS AND SUBCONSCIOUS MIND

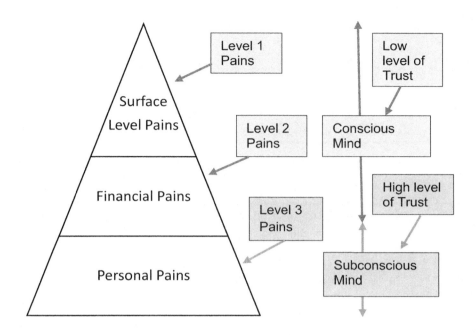

FIGURE 8: THE DIFFERENT LEVELS OF PAIN AND WHERE THEY RESIDE.
THE SURFACE AND FINANCIAL PAINS MOSTLY LIVE IN CONSCIOUS MIND,
WHEREAS THE PERSONAL PAINS PRIMARILY RESIDE IN THE
SUBCONSCIOUS MIND.

Now we present four different examples of surface level pains, the associated financial pains and the resultant personal pains in the same order. It is evident from figure that for each surface level pain, there are associated financial and personal pains as shown in Figure 9.

This is the third time I am repairing these windows

I am fed up by the internet connection, it just gets disconnected all the time

I could not get a pay raise though I deserved it.

The garbage collectors are never on time and the filled garbage smell bad.

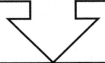

The window repairs have cost me a over 300 GBP already.

I am losing money since I am an internet marketer and the internet connection problems have cost me over 3K GBP due to the clients which switched to competitors

The pay raise would have enabled me to generate an extra 20K per year.

We have to pay another garbage collector twice "and this costs has costed me a fortune".

The windows get broken quite often and the cold air enters the room. Due to this, I cannot sleep and it has affected my well-being.

Since I have lost loyal customer, I cannot focus on creative work.That has resulted in self-doubt, loss of confidence and I feel as if I am lagging behind the competitors.

I cannot send my son to a good private school due to the same salary. I worked hard for the promotion and I cannot sleep because of it.

I have a home office and the clients who visit me have pointed it out. Two have never returned and it has resulted in arguments between me and wife and it is emotioanally draining.

Figure 9: An example of four surface level pains, their associated financial pains and the resulting personal pains in the same order.

CHAPTER 21

Three Levels of Gaps

In this chapter, we are going to explore the gaps which prospects have between their desired future state and the current state. The current state is defined in terms of the three levels of pains which must be overcome to reach a desired future state. The future state also consists of three levels. The topmost level consists of the improvement in their business or their lives when a solution to Level 1 problem is obtained. The second level of future state consists of the improvement in the financial situation after the Level 2 problem is mitigated. The third level of future state consists of the desired emotional state of the prospect when the Level 3 problems are reduced or eliminated. I call the three levels of future state the vision pyramid.

The pain pyramid is, therefore, a representation of where the prospects currently are due to their problems when seen through the lens of intellect, finances and emotions. On the other hand, the vision pyramid describes the vision which prospects paint during a closing conversation. It is a dreamland where the prospects want to be in future. After painting this picture, the prospect realises the gap and becomes aware of the gap. The prospects paint the picture on their own, and a closer merely facilitates them in painting it by asking the right questions as described in section 5 and section 6 of the book.

Hence, the vision pyramid shows where they want to be after their problems are solved at all levels, i.e., intellectual, financial and emotional. Even though the emotional gap is the most important, thinking about the gap at three different levels will help you visualise the way your solution will transform their lives at the emotional level, solve their business problem at the topmost level and improve the financial dimension in the middle level. Your job as a closer is to uncover the gap at each level by asking the right questions. They will help you paint the vision (or, define the vision pyramid) during conversation.

In this way, your prospects will close themselves instead of you closing them. Once the gap is clearly revealed at each level by the prospects, you can then tell them how your service will help them reach the desired future state, or how their problem will be solved or subsided significantly via your product or service. The aforementioned concepts are summarised in Figure 10.

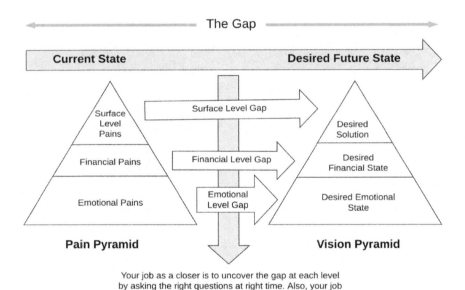

Your job as a closer is to uncover the gap at each level by asking the right questions at right time. Also, your job is is to ask questoins which will help them in painting a picture of their desired future state (vision pyramid).

FIGURE 10: A VISUAL REPRESENTATION OF THE THREE LEVELS OF GAP. THE CURRENT STATE IS DESCRIBED BY THE PAIN PYRAMID AND THE DESIRED FUTURE STATE IS REPRESENTED BY THE VISION PYRAMID.

Based on my experience as a closer, here are the key points which I believe are very important to remember. These key concepts will act in your favour and help you close with confidence.

1. Remember that the prospect stays in their current state because they are not able to solve the problem on his own.

2. Your product or service acts as the train which will take the prospects to their destination (the desired future state). Before they access your product or service, they were waiting for the train in frustration. You, as a closer, act as the event "arrival of the train." Your call will help them step on the train, meaning access your product or service. Now they can reach their destination, "the desired future state," by covering the distance to their destination, thereby "filling the gap." The time which they spent inside the train represents "the time during which the prospect was using the product or service (the train)."

3. If the prospect was able to fill the gap by himself, he wouldn't be on the phone with you.

4. Therefore, it is crucial for you to understand that your product or service has no worth whatsoever if it cannot fill the gap which the customer currently has. This means that they are not actually buying your product or service, but buying their way out of something. That "something" is the gap. Hence, instead of talking about your product's features and benefits, you should focus on the gap and thoroughly understand it at all levels. During the last stage, you can describe the way your product or service will bridge the gap. Once you know this critical point, the sales conversations will become effortless. You don't have to sell your product or service anymore; you will instead sell the way your service or product gives the prospect "ways out" of their current state to their desired future state.

5. Sometimes the prospects are not ready, which means that the emotional pains are not so severe, and they are not hungry enough to change their current state, or the gap is not that important to them. That is perfectly fine, as I say:

Prospects take action to reach their desired state when the cost of staying in the current state is more than the cost of filling the gap.

—Subayal

6. At the end of the sale conversation, if you find that the prospects are not ready, it is fine since the impact of their problems might not be enough to motivate them to take action.

7. Sometimes, closers fail to understand the current state and the gap. If they are not able to reveal the pains, they won't be able to close the sale. These skills will sharpen as you practice more and do more roleplays, as mentioned in section 6.

It is not about the sales script; it is about the underlying flow and mechanics of a sales conversation!

—Subayal

SECTION 7:

STEP 5: ANATOMY OF SALES CLOSING COVERSATION

CHAPTER 22

The Underlying Mechanics

Rapport and Trust

Remember that trust which builds as a result of rapport is vital. If the client doesn't trust you, they won't buy from you. You know "people always buy people" before they purchase the products and services from them. So, building trust is crucial.

To build trust, you have to listen and acknowledge the things that the prospect is saying which will help you see things from their perspective. The prospects have found their way to you via a webinar, funnel, YouTube video, Facebook ad, TV ad, press release or other form of advertising. They are on the call with you because they want your solution. Your main objective is to make them feel understood, get them emotionally involved, build trust, and uncover their pains. With this approach, you will know the severity of their problems, and also help them in unlocking their vision.

You achieve the aforementioned objectives by asking them the right questions at the right time during a conversation. When you ask questions, you must listen carefully and focus. It will help you understand their pains better. After detecting some pains, you can ask further questions which will reveal even more pains. In this way, you will understand the impact of discovered problems on their business and life. When you listen with intent and ask the right questions, they will explain the impact of their problems and pains from various angles. The discussion above can be described in one sentence:

When you hear them but don't listen to them, you cannot reveal the impact of their pains.

—Subayal

Once you have thoroughly understood their problem, you can tell the prospect how your solution will mitigate their problems. In this way, they will see why your solution is the right one for them, and in which ways it can help them solve their problems. Remember that a sale closing call is about them and not about you. Also, that they will only share their limiting beliefs, anxieties, fears, emotions and feelings with you only and only if:

1. **You have a sincere intent.**

2. **You care about them.**

3. **You direct your emotional energy to understand their problems.**

4. **You listen to them like a doctor.**

5. **You ask questions with an intent to help them overcome their challenges.**

6. **You have understood their personality well and adjusted your tonality accordingly.**

7. **You radiate empathy and have a desire to help them.**

8. **You are not self-centred, and you don't sound or feel like a typical salesperson whom everyone dislikes.**

The points mentioned above will mitigate friction, objections and develop trust. They will also help you dig deeper and see the way their problems are impacting them emotionally, which is very important for closing a sale.

Maintaining Control

Whoever asks the questions during a sales conversation maintains control of the conversation. So, if you ask questions, you will have the control of conversation, but if the prospect starts asking questions, the ball goes to their court and the prospect gets control of the conversation.

When you have lost control of the conversation, you have lost the sale.

—Subayal

From my experience, I have seen that when a sales conversation starts, the first goal should be to build a rapport with the prospect. Rapport can be built by asking prospects general questions about their situation. Also, at this stage, you can tell them a little about yourself. Building rapport is described in detail in section six and is very important to build trust and making your prospect feel safe.

Once the initial trust is established and they feel safe, mention with finesse that to understand their current state and challenges you would like to ask some questions so that you can see whether you can help overcome their challenges. This is imperative, because until you have understood their problem, you are never going to make a sale. Also, clients always want to be understood.

During a closing call, when they ask you a question, you should always ask a question in response to maintain control of the call. Also, after building rapport, you must pre-frame the conversation in such a way that they agree and permit you to ask them questions.

It will help you maintain the control of conversation. Let us pretend that you are closing a personal transformation program for an influencer; you can pre-frame the call by saying something like:

"You know that our programs are related to personal transformation. Therefore, to see whether it would be a right fit for you, we would like to ask you some questions to understand how your inner world looks. In this way, we will know whether we can help you transform your inner world. We know that we cannot help everyone, so if it is the right fit for you, we will tell you, and if it is not the right fit, we will also inform you. So, is it okay if we ask you some questions?"

They always say "yes" in response and permit you to ask questions. So far, in 12 years I got a "no" just 4 times. In all these cases, I said: "then I cannot help you." Right after that, they allowed me to ask them questions.

Once you have pre-framed the call, you can ask questions with finesse and steer the conversation from time to time to uncover their pains, allow them to solve the problem themselves and also help them paint a picture of the life which they want after going through the personal transformation program. Once you have understood their problems and the future state which they long for, you can ask questions so that they close themselves on the gap. Also, by asking questions, you can mitigate the resistance from the prospect and stay focused on diagnosing the current state of the prospect to uncover the pains which they have.

> *Closing is an art of steering the conversion in the right direction, at the right time, with the right intent and right tonality by asking the right questions.*
>
> *—Subayal*

Whoever asked the questions, controls the conversation. If the prospect is asking the questions, they will look like this:

What is the price?

What are the features of your product/service?

And so on.

Therefore, if the prospects ask questions and control the conversation, the main objective of the conversation, which is to understand their problems, goes into the background. To mitigate this situation, we ask questions in response to questions and this technique is called *redirection*. So, for example, when the client asks you about the product features or benefits, tell them, "We will go into the product features and benefits later because we have a lot of different products or different services, and right now we don't know which products would be a right for you. So, to go into the product features, we first have to understand your needs. We first have to understand the challenges that you are facing." Remember that the closing call is about them, not about your product or services. It will help if you never start discussing product features and benefits until you believe that they will contribute to closing the sale and benefit the prospect.

Uncovering the pains

I remember walking in the Christmas market when my two-and-a-half-year-old son started to dance to music played by an armature band. He was having the time of his life and couldn't stop smiling, when he suddenly saw an ice-cream truck and the cute little man showed me his true colours. His smiles turned into anger, and the dance moves turned into protest jumps. I saw a lady and asked her, "Can you kindly tell me where I can find a store to buy some ice cream?" She showed me the way. I begged my son to stop crying, but he wouldn't listen. In the end, he agreed to sit in the stroller, and we soon ended up in a store where we bought the ice cream. But he wouldn't stop crying.

Now that was tough, and I didn't understand how I can help him. When I asked him: What does he want? He said ice cream, but it was in his hands. I asked him again. You have the ice cream already, what do you want. He said, "ice cream truck". Now I understood that he wanted ice cream for sure, but he wanted the one sold by an ice cream truck. He did not like the same chocolate bar from a boring shop which he loves. For over 40 minutes this nightmare continued, and I prayed to God, "Ice cream truck please." After walking for 20 more minutes in sub-zero temperatures, I was hopeless until I saw another ice cream truck parked a hundred metres away on the side of a road. My hands were frozen, but I was relieved. My son was so happy and delighted that as soon as he came out of the stroller, he rushed to the ice cream truck. He started dancing to the music of the truck when he reached it and bought the same ice cream which we purchased from the shop. He was so happy and delighted that he danced for 5 minutes straight and the truck owner enjoyed his dance moves.

The conclusion of the story is that *"I uncovered the emotional pain of my son, which resulted due to the deprivation of experience which he craved for."*

The ice cream was the same, but the experience that he wanted was different. I uncovered his pain by asking his two questions. When we grow up, we are no different, and that is why we crave for luxury and experience, which will help us get the emotions that we desire. In the same way, when you ask questions with an intent to throw light on the different aspects of professional or personal lives of prospects, you will uncover their pains. If you master this craft, you will achieve incredible results and help prospects in solving their problems.

The pains related to different aspects of their life ultimately affect their emotional state, which they want to change!

—Subayal

If prospects are not able to realise the severity of their pains and the impact which they are having on their lives, the sale will not happen. You must help them by revealing the way these pains are affecting their lives. When these pains are revealed, the prospects get emotionally involved, which is very important for the closing the sale.

> *A sale is only closed when the prospects are emotionally involved.*
>
> *—Subayal*

Another critical point here is that you should focus on open-ended questions so that they can explain to you their situation in their own words while replying to your questions. When you ask open-ended questions, they open up, and they will tell you more details. As we say, "the devil is in the details," and likewise, the pains of prospects are also in the details about their current situations which they tell you when you ask open-ended questions.

You should talk less and listen more so that you can note down their pains as the conversation unfolds. Also, you can ask further questions to uncover more pains until you have painted a picture of their current state. If you have successfully painted a picture of their current state, it means you have already developed enough trust with the prospect, and they are emotionally involved. Afterwards, you can ask them further questions so that they can paint a picture of the state that they want to reach.

The next step is to help them identify the different levels of gaps and the different levels of pains which are described in section four. The last two steps include costing the problem and helping them understand the way they can reach their desired state by utilizing your product or service. In the end, you close the sale as described in section six.

Costing the Problem and Consequence

During a sales conversation, you will get price objections if the prospects have not revealed the financial cost which the problem is having. The prospects must tell you themselves how much will it cost them if they won't take action and solve the problem which they are having. The reason is that "When they say it, they own it." They must know that remaining in the current state is costing them more than the cost of solving the problem. If they know it, they will purchase the product or service which will help them solve their problem. This will help you eliminate price objections. I help the prospects in costing the problem in two steps.

Step 1: Pre-Costing, or "Realisation of Importance":

Before costing the problem, you have to do some work. Meaning you should help them realise that the problem is worth solving.

When you ask the prospect: Why was he not able to solve the problem on his own? What are they going to tell you? They are going to tell you the reasons why they were not able to solve this problem on their own. Now, you can also ask them what other programs, services, products or training which they used, utilized or attended to solve the problem on their own? And also, why did they not work?

In this way, they will tell you themselves the reasons why they were unsuccessful before, due to which they came on the phone call with you. It means that they are themselves answering the questions: Why do they need this solution so urgently? And, why is it so important to them to take action now?

You can also ask them: What would happen if you don't take any action to solve this problem? And how likely it is that they will be able to solve the problem on their own? And once again they will tell you about the services and products which they tried. Also, you can ask them: Why were they not able to solve the problem after using the products and services which they mentioned? This helps you understand the shortcomings of competitors, which you can leverage in the last step of the closing call. Remember that you should not try to explicitly compare, but rather mention with finesse the way you will help the prospect in solving these problems. Maintain the focus on the prospect's problem and not competition; otherwise, they will start thinking about you as a traditional salesman. Also, two other questions which I usually ask are: How long has this problem lasted? And how it has impacted them until now, and in which ways?

As a closer, you want the prospects to convince themselves that they need your solution and they must take action now.

—Subayal

Also, remember that:

The more they themselves emphasize the importance and urgency of a solution, the more likely the sale!

—Subayal

Step 2: Costing

After doing the background work in Step 1, the stage is set for costing the problem which will help the prospects realise that taking action is the right way to go since there is a financial cost attached to the current state. This cost is more than the cost of the solution which you are offering. Here, you have to ask the prospect: What would happen if they did not take action?

You can also ask questions like: What would happen, if you are not able to solve your problem? How much do you think it is going to cost your business? Or, how much do you think it is going to impact your finances?

Once they tell you that it is going to cost them, for example, ten thousand dollars a month or a thousand dollars a month, it means that they subconsciously agree that the solution is worth paying. The solution is worth paying for since it costs less than what it costs for them to remain in the same state.

At the end of the sales conversation when you bring up the price, you will most likely have no price objection. If you do, you can refer to the additional cost which they have to pay if they stay where they are.

Therefore, costing the problem is one of the most critical techniques to eliminate price objections. When they themselves have said how much the problem is costing them, the price objections evaporate.

CHAPTER 23

Clarity, Conviction and Confidence

During a sale closing conversation, a salesperson must ask the right questions at the right time to uncover the pain pyramid, the vision pyramid and the three levels of gaps so that the prospects feel understood and take an informed purchasing decision. To accomplish and ensure that, a sales conversation process is developed which consists of six stages. If followed correctly, the prospect gets conviction, clarity and confidence during a sales conversation since they get a clear picture of their goals, challenges, priorities and desires. In short, your role as a sale closer is to come from a position to serve and your sincere intent should be to help them. When you radiate this positive energy, the prospects connect to you at an emotional level and feel that you are trustworthy.

Moreover, their level of urgency can be gauged by asking them the right questions to uncover their past efforts to make this change. That will, in turn, help you in gauging their level of commitment to making the change in their business or lives.

As you build the rapport and show interest in understanding their problem, it enhances their trust on you and your solution. At the end of sales conversation, they can, therefore, gauge themselves: How aligned your value proposition is with their objectives, wants, desires?

In short, by answering your questions at different stages of a sale closing conversation mentioned in next chapter, you help them in taking the best decision for themselves so that they can overcome their challenges and realise their vision of a problem-free future. This indicates that closing is not something which you do to a prospect, but it is something which you do for the prospect. You facilitate the prospect in making the well-informed decision themselves.

When you come from a position of problem solver and you intend to serve the prospect, you will close more sales than traditional salespersons. This is exactly the goal of different stages of the sales conversation process mentioned in the next chapter. This process makes sure that the prospect gets clarity, conviction and confidence about various important points mentioned in Table 6.

TABLE 6: THE THREE CS OF A SALE CLOSING CONVERSATION AND IMPORTANT POINTS UNDERPINNED BY EACH C.

Three Cs: A Prospect Must Have Each of Them at The End of a Sale Closing Conversation.	Important Points Underpinning Each "C".
1. Clarity	1. On Their Goals 2. On Their Challenges 3. On Their Priorities 4. On Their Wants/Pains
2. Conviction	1. Your Service/Product Is Right for Them 2. You Are Trustworthy 3. This Is the Time to Act 4. That They Commit to The Process or Are Willing to Make the Change
3. Confidence	1. In Your Expertise/Service Offering 2. It Is Aligned with Their Objectives/Wants/Desires

CHAPTER 24

The Flow and Stages

While talking to many good closers, I have found that quite often the influencers or businesses provide them with scripts which they want them to read to the prospects over the phone. This is the most efficient way to obliterate rapport and reduce the closing rate. On the flip side, those closers who use a structure with proper stages in their closing calls are the most successful. Some call it the "flow," and some refer to this as the "blueprint," while some even call it the "script."

The main objective of such a structure *with proper stages* is to illustrate and define the flow of a sales conversation clearly. We will elaborate on each stage in this chapter and describe each of these stages in detail in the next chapter. As you can see, trust is the most critical element of a sales closing conversation. When trust is established at the beginning of the conversation, it makes the communication smooth, and as a result, the prospects easily share their challenges, problems and pains with you.

1. Trust and making them feel safe

Establish trust, adjust tonality and know their personality.

2. Agenda

Frame the call so that you can move towards the exploration and discovery phase.

3. Exploration and discovery

Ask questions to uncover pains and the gap. Listen and write down pain points as they reveal their pains in response to your questions. The three levels of pains are identified during this phase.

Listen more and talk less during this phase. Ask open-ended questions so that you can gather more information about their pains.

4. Gap clarification

In this phase, the three levels of gaps are found which are described by the prospects as they answer your questions. You facilitate them in elaborating the gap by asking the right questions, with the right tonality and with finesse.

5. Prospect Gap-Selling

Ask questions so that the prospects can themselves sell the gap.

6. Close by matching features with desires.

Match the features to their vision and close. In the next chapter, we describe all the stages in detail.

CHAPTER 25

Dissecting the Stages

In this chapter, we elaborate each element of the sales conversation flow in detail in order to develop a deep understanding of the purpose and underlying intent as well as the encompassing objectives. I firmly believe that it is fundamentally important to understand the reasons why each one of these stages exists and what lies beneath the surface at each stage. That develops a conviction and trust in the process. Knowing these stages at the surface will not take you far, but knowing them in depth will enable you to refine and adapt them in various scenarios. It will make you a top-notch closer in any industry if you remain consistent and trust in the process. Also, it means that you don't need to read human psychology in-depth, but you still need to understand the way a particular stage contributes to the flow of a sales closing conversation. That not only reduces the time and effort but also gives you confidence by producing consistent results, and that is what matters at the end of the day. After 12 years of closing experience, I came up with the flow and structure shown in Table 7, and I use it during every sales closing call. In the next chapter, I have provided the blueprint script, which consists of questions I ask during each stage of a sales closing conversation. It is very flexible and can be applied in any scenario.

TABLE 7: FLOW AND STRUCTURE OF A SALES CONVERSATION WHICH I DEVELOPED, AND THESE STAGES EXPLAINED IN DETAIL.

Elements and flow	Purpose, Description and strategy of each phase.
Stage 1: Trust and making them feel safe:	**Why rapport is so critical:** The first few seconds of the call matter immensely. If the prospect feels that there is a disconnect between both parties, you may have already lost

Dissecting the main elements of a rapport.	the sale. Creating a connection helps to set the atmosphere. It also puts the prospect at ease and in a better mindset to answer your questions. **Checking social media to get to know them:** Before you go deep into the call, get started on informing yourself about the prospect, e.g. via Facebook, YouTube, homepage etc. and find out if he/she has hobbies, family, interests etc. that you can rely on and build a personal connection. With this step, you will be able to earn trust and confidence. This is essential in order to close the sale over the phone at the end of the conversation. Put a good vibe into the conversation and also laugh together. You've got to keep it real. Be genuine. Then frame the call. Connect. Build trust. It doesn't need to feel fake. People can tell when you are really connecting. Before the call, look them up on Facebook, and do a little homework on them so you can genuinely connect. Do this until you connect even if it takes an hour. Sometimes it will only take 5 minutes. **Know which gem they are in the first few seconds:** Mirror her/him – which GEM is she/he – I fall in love with my customer's outcome. 1. **Sapphire: Fast and excited, loud-speaker – motivated by fun, party, good times** 2. **Pearl: Calm speakers, driven by helping other people, not by money, loyal, friendly, love people, personal, fulfilment, connect emotionally, lower voice, hear them and listen with the intent** 3. **Emerald: Motivated by facts and figures, detailed, precise, very organized, loyal, helpful, they need information, more driven & business-like, process-oriented,**

they view things black & white and do things in a step by step manner.

4. Ruby: Motivated by a challenge or money, risk-takers, go-getters, ambitious, competitive, winners, don´t go into too many details

Some important points:

1. Understand their personality and shift your vocal tone to match.

2. You want to become their friend.

3. Be someone who wants to help them, instead of someone who wants to sell them.

4. You are a supporter, someone to trust, someone who cares about their family, hobbies and goals, not a pesky salesman/woman.

What do you want to secure during rapport?

Notes - You want to secure [Name, Location, Reason for calling, Insight into goals/problems] + TRUST + CONNECTION WITH THEM. Always use their name during the call.

Connect and Build Trust:

You've got to keep it real. Be genuine. Then frame the call. Connect. Build trust. It doesn't need to feel fake. People can tell when you are really connecting. Before the call, look them up on Facebook, do a little homework on them so you can genuinely connect. Do this until you connect even if it takes an hour. Sometimes it will only take 5 minutes. Use their name constantly throughout the call.

Additional vital points to remember:

	1. You are here to help, and not to scare.
	2. Don't sound as if you are here to cash in on their problems.
	3. You first must think like a friend and act as if you are helping them.
	4. The people in management/CEOs/COOs, etc., will understand these signals, and it will be very awkward and feel wrong.
Stage 2: Agenda "Frame the call" so that you can move towards the Exploration.	The main goals of this step are to frame the call in such a way that you can ask the questions in the third step, i.e., the exploration step. You get the prospect, *implicitly* and *with finesse*, to agree with the point that you are here to understand their current state. Your aim is to get their approval of asking the questions which will eventually lead to uncovering their pains by them. Without this step, they might not actually like the questions or perceive them as awkward. When they have agreed with you on that, they own their decision and this implicitly motivates them to answer your questions and direct their energy to the answers, since they know the purpose behind that.

You can ask questions like these. But please, do not memorize them, and use tonality to your advantage. Use your own words, and sound genuine. Your intent will radiate, and the prospects will feel it. You can never ever fake your intention and the sincere desire to help them solve their problems. Be a facilitator and focus on them, not yourself and your product or service. Here is a set of questions which I use, but you can create your own so that they reflect your personality, not mine.

1. **PROSPECT**, I really want to be respectful of your time. In order to ensure that you get the maximum |

value out of this call, we need to get clarity on why you called and understand your current challenges.

2. So, during this call, we will discover whether this program is the right fit for you, and if we find that it is the case, we will tell you!

3. And if we find that it is not the right fit for you, we will also inform you. Either way, you'll get massive value and clarity!

4. **PROSPECT** Just before we get into that can I double-check that you have 45 minutes scheduled for this call?

5. So, in order to find whether we can help you, I will ask you some questions. Is that okay with you?

Stage 3: Exploration and discovery Ask questions to uncover pains and the gap. Listen to write down pain points as they reveal their pains in response to your questions. Here are the objectives of this phase: Three levels of pains identified. Level three pains found.	The aim of this phase is to uncover the pains at each level and get a thorough understanding of the problems which together forge their current state. This phase should not sound like an interview. You should ask questions with finesse and keep on taking the pains at different levels by taking notes. You should note down as much of their pains as possible at different levels during the exploration and discovery process. **Uncover the pains at each of the three levels:** You have to dive more deeply than what is obvious. Get past the superficial problems. There's usually a REAL problem where people go, "Wow. I never thought about that. Wow, I never thought it was affecting my life. Wow, I never thought that was a problem." **Probe like a doctor:** Drive and probe like an attorney or doctor. It will be malpractice if we don't ask the right questions. How did it happen? How long

Listen more and talk less during this phase!

Ask open-ended questions.

ago? Let's get some x-rays and take a look under the hood.

Don't coach and become information broker: The goal is not to give them what they want—they might wish for free information (a Band-Aid). If someone has a stage 4 cancer, you CAN'T provide them with a Band-Aid (which usually comes free) or hope without treating it. A lot of clients think they don't have that last piece of info or secret that has made it click. The real reason is they haven't made the DECISION to change—the people who buy a million books on a topic but never really work on it. Information seekers don't FIX the problem with information.

Your role as a closer: We are here to serve them, and the only way we can help them is to get them to make a decision to FIX it. When they know the severity and impact of the problems, they will say, "Oh no, no more, I am done. Where do I sign up?" This is where we want them to be.

Don't be too caring to keep them in current state: If you are also caring by nature, you may have a compassionate tendency to say oh it's not that bad, you're doing better than others…softening it or going into consultant mode to solve. DON'T SOFTEN AND DON'T SOLVE. That is not in the best interest of your prospect because he or she has a problem that is urgent and worth solving, due to which they are on phone call with you. If you act as a coach, they might think that it is not worth solving, and as a result, they will keep on having the surface level, financial and emotional pains. They must take action to solve their problem, and in order for them to take action, they must understand the impact of their problems from various angles. This is precisely the goal of this phase.

Important points to consider during this step:

	1. During exploration of pains, sound helpful, don't scare, say things like "It could be due to ...reason1 ...reason2 ..." or "It might be due to ...reason1 ...reason2..." or "maybe you could have done ...action1 ...action2" and always behave like a close friend.
	2. Use their name consistently throughout the call.
	3. Avoid the "umm" sound during conversation, don't get very excited and avoid saying things like "Yeah, this program ... " Also, don't use the word "great" too often.
Stage 4: Gap clarification The three levels of gap found	In this book, the gap clarification step focuses on helping the prospect paint a picture of their ideal future state at some point in the future by asking the right questions in the same way as in the previous phase. Sometimes I merge that phase with the exploration phase, since you will still be asking questions and uncovering where their desired future state lies, and what would be the ideal solution to their problems at a point in future, after 3, 4 or 5 years of months depending on the industry and the problems. The future state which they desire is also called the vision, and they can paint the vision for you if you ask the right questions. Remember they should paint the picture of the vision "future state" for you and this will only happen if you ask them the right questions. *Note: Do not ask question like these since they can harm your credibility as an expert. You should know the solution, not them. Also, in most cases, the prospects don't know the solution, and if they had known what to do, they wouldn't be on the phone with you in the first place.*

	Avoid these questions at all costs: 1. What would be the best solution to your problem? 2. What would be the most "scalable, reliable, long-term, adaptive, agile or viable" solution which will take your business to the next level? 3. What would be the best way to align your current business process to the market demands? 4. What adjustments do you think are necessary to target your ads to the right audience? 5. What type of refinement to your services will keep your services unmatched in this market segment after six months, one year or another time frame? **Note:** You can form your own questions and practice them via roleplays. You don't need to memorize them. The main idea is to help you understand the way a closing conversation is carried out.
Stage 5: Prospect Gap-Selling Ask questions so that they sell themselves	In this step, your job is to do the groundwork by helping the prospect sell themselves on the gap. Meaning the prospects should tell you themselves during this step the reasons why they must act now. Once they sell themselves, this will mitigate objections since they themselves will tell you how urgent it is and how much it costs them. After this phase, the prospect has sold himself on the idea that filling the gap is essential. Therefore, this phase is called "prospect gap-selling." *"The future state which they desire is also called the vision."*

	After revealing the desired future state, discover: How urgent is it to reach that state? How much will it cost them? How important it is for their bottom line to get a solution and reach there? How much can it cost them during the time that passes monthly, quarterly, or yearly if they do not find a solution?
Stage 6: Close "match features and desires." Match the features to their vision Close the prospect.	**In this step, help them understand:** How your solution is going to help them in solving their problem and How your solution will provide them with the missing features, technology, mindset (in personal development B2C context), knowledge, frameworks and techniques etc., provided by you or your firm help them in going from the current state to their desired state. Once that is done, you ask them whether they want to go ahead and take action or not! **Note:** *Don't be pushy, don't become attached to the sale and only focus on solving their problem. This pattern interrupt will serve you very well. In other words, the more you sound, act and behave in contradiction with a stereotypical salesman, the better your chances of making a sale.*

Without clarity and conviction, you won't stay motivated in the long run and won't achieve greatness.

—Subayal

SECTION 8:

STEP6:
THE BLUEPRINTS

CHAPTER 26

Blueprint: The Generic Script

One thing which I often come across is that many sales experts emphasize the need to ask questions. But the actual reality is different, since it is not just about having a bunch of questions or using a fixed script on each sales closing call. Surely, generic scripts can be used as a guide which will help you visualize: What went through the mind of a top-notch closer who developed it? You have to be genuine, and you must express yourself in your own unique words during a sales closing call. Hence, the script mentioned here is a reflection of who I am and how I think. It lists the questions which I ask the prospects in my own words. You can definitely use this flow and the sequence of steps.

One of the most important things during a sales closing conversation is listening. When you listen to the prospect, you note down the pain points, and afterwards, you ask further probing questions with finesse, meaning, without sounding like an interviewer. This will help you in also exploring the pains at lower levels. Hence, you can only ask the right questions when you listen. Therefore, instead of sounding like a typical salesperson who cannot stop talking about the features of his product or service, you listen and focus on understanding their problem. Of course, understanding is all about uncovering the pain at all three levels, meaning what your prospect is going through at an intellectual level, financial level, and emotional level due to the problem which motivated him to be on the phone with you today.

After elaborating the different steps of a sales closing conversation, I now provide a generic blueprint script. This blueprint script can be modified or fine-tuned to your industry. This blueprint mainly describes the questions which you can potentially ask at each step of a sales conversation. This blueprint will help you ask these or similar questions in your own words. The underlying motive of each step has been described in section 5. In this blueprint script, I have mentioned the questions in each step which I myself ask during a sales closing conversation. You can write these questions in your own words so that you sound genuine. The more real and authentic you sound, the more people will improve your results.

As you do more roleplays, you will find other questions which you can note down and write in each step. In this way, your version of blueprint script will grow with time. It will contain more questions for handling different situations. The generic script that acts as a blueprint and can be adapted to various situations is presented in Table 8.

TABLE 8: A GENERIC SCRIPT WHICH ACTS AS A BLUEPRINT THAT CAN BE ADAPTED TO VARIOUS CONTEXTS, FOR EXAMPLE, B2B, B2C OR DIFFERENT INDUSTRIES.

Elements and flow	Purpose, Description and strategy of each phase.
Stage 1: Trust and making them feel safe: Dissecting the main elements of a rapport.	**Why rapport is so critical:** The first few seconds of the call matter immensely. If the prospect feels that there is a disconnect between both parties, you may have already lost the sale. Creating a connection helps to set the atmosphere. It also puts the prospect at ease and in a better mindset to answer your questions. **Checking social media to get to know them:** Before you go deep into the call, get started on informing yourself about the prospect, e.g. via Facebook, YouTube, homepage etc. and find out if he/she has hobbies, family, interests etc. that you can rely on and build a personal connection. With this step, you will be able to earn trust and confidence. This is essential in order to close the

sale over the phone at the end of the conversation. Put a good vibe into the conversation and also laugh together. You've got to keep it real. Be genuine. Then frame the call. Connect. Build trust. It doesn't need to feel fake. People can tell when you are really connecting. Before the call, look them up on Facebook, and do a little homework on them so you can genuinely connect. Do this until you connect even if it takes an hour. Sometimes it will only take 5 minutes.

Know which gem they are in the first few seconds:

Mirror her/him – which GEM is she/he – I fall in love with my customer's outcome.

1. **Sapphire: Fast and excited, loud-speaker – motivated by fun, party, good times**

2. **Pearl: Calm speakers, driven by helping other people, not by money, loyal, friendly, love people, personal, fulfilment, connect emotionally, lower voice, hear them and listen with the intent**

3. **Emerald: Motivated by facts and figures, detailed, precise, very organized, loyal, helpful, they need information, more driven & business-like, process-oriented, they view things black & white and do things in a step by step manner.**

4. **Ruby: Motivated by a challenge or money, risk-takers, go-getters, ambitious, competitive, winners, don´t go into too many details**

Some important points:

1. **Understand their personality and shift your vocal tone to match.**

2. You want to become their friend.

3. Be someone who wants to help them, instead of someone who wants to sell them.

4. You are a supporter, someone to trust, someone who cares about their family, hobbies and goals, not a pesky salesman/woman.

What do you want to secure during rapport?

Notes - You want to secure [Name, Location, Reason for calling, Insight into goals/problems] + TRUST + CONNECTION WITH THEM. Always use their name during the call.

Connect and Build Trust:

You've got to keep it real. Be genuine. Then frame the call. Connect. Build trust. It doesn't need to feel fake. People can tell when you are really connecting. Before the call, look them up on Facebook, do a little homework on them so you can genuinely connect. Do this until you connect even if it takes an hour. Sometimes it will only take 5 minutes. Use their name constantly throughout the call.

Additional vital points to remember:

1. You are here to help, and not to scare.

2. Don't sound as if you are here to cash in on their problems.

3. You first must think like a friend and act as if you are helping them.

4. The people in management/CEOs/COOs, etc., will understand these signals, and it will be very awkward and feel wrong.

Stage 2: Agenda "Frame the call" so that you can move towards the Exploration.	The main goals of this step are to frame the call in such a way that you can ask the questions in the third step, i.e., the exploration step. You get the prospect, *implicitly* and *with finesse*, to agree with the point that you are here to understand their current state. Your aim is to get their approval of asking the questions which will eventually lead to uncovering their pains by them. Without this step, they might not actually like the questions or perceive them as awkward. When they have agreed with you on that, they own their decision and this implicitly motivates them to answer your questions and direct their energy to the answers, since they know the purpose behind that. You can ask questions like these. But please, do not memorize them, and use tonality to your advantage. Use your own words, and sound genuine. Your intent will radiate, and the prospects will feel it. You can never ever fake your intention and the sincere desire to help them solve their problems. Be a facilitator and focus on them, not yourself and your product or service. Here is a set of questions which I use, but you can create your own so that they reflect your personality, not mine. 1. **PROSPECT**, I really want to be respectful of your time. In order to ensure that you get the maximum value out of this call, we need to get clarity on why you called and understand your current challenges. 2. So, during this call, we will discover whether this program is the right fit for you, and if we find that it is the case, we will tell you! 3. And if we find that it is not the right fit for you, we will also inform you. Either way, you'll get massive value and clarity!

	4. **PROSPECT** Just before we get into that can I double-check that you have 45 minutes scheduled for this call? 5. So, in order to find whether we can help you, I will ask you some questions. Is that okay with you?
Stage 3: Exploration and discovery Ask questions to uncover pains and the gap. Listen to write down pain points as they reveal their pains in response to your questions. Here are the objectives of this phase: Three levels of pains identified. Level three pains found. Listen more and talk less during this phase! Ask open-ended questions.	The aim of this phase is to uncover the pains at each level and get a thorough understanding of the problems which together forge their current state. This phase should not sound like an interview. You should ask questions with finesse and keep on taking the pains at different levels by taking notes. You should note down as much of their pains as possible at different levels during the exploration and discovery process. **Uncover the pains at each of the three levels:** You have to dive more deeply than what is obvious. Get past the superficial problems. There's usually a REAL problem where people go, "Wow. I never thought about that. Wow, I never thought it was affecting my life. Wow, I never thought that was a problem." **Probe like a doctor:** Drive and probe like an attorney or doctor. It will be malpractice if we don't ask the right questions. How did it happen? How long ago? Let's get some x-rays and take a look under the hood. **Don't coach and become information broker:** The goal is not to give them what they want—they might wish for free information (a Band-Aid). If someone has a stage 4 cancer, you CAN'T provide them with a Band-Aid (which usually comes free) or hope without treating it. A lot of clients think they don't have that last piece of info or secret that has made it click. The real reason is they haven't made the DECISION to change—the people who buy a million books on a

topic but never really work on it. Information seekers don't FIX the problem with information.

Your role as a closer: We are here to serve them, and the only way we can help them is to get them to make a decision to FIX it. When they know the severity and impact of the problems, they will say, "Oh no, no more, I am done. Where do I sign up?" This is where we want them to be.

Don't be too caring to keep them in current state: If you are also caring by nature, you may have a compassionate tendency to say oh it's not that bad, you're doing better than others…softening it or going into consultant mode to solve. DON'T SOFTEN AND DON'T SOLVE. That is not in the best interest of your prospect because he or she has a problem that is urgent and worth solving, due to which they are on phone call with you. If you act as a coach, they might think that it is not worth solving, and as a result, they will keep on having the surface level, financial and emotional pains. They must take action to solve their problem, and in order for them to take action, they must understand the impact of their problems from various angles. This is precisely the goal of this phase.

Important points to consider during this step:

1. During exploration of pains, sound helpful, don't scare, say things like "It could be due to …reason1 …reason2 …" or "It might be due to …reason1 …reason2…" or "maybe you could have done …action1 …action2" and always behave like a close friend.

2. Use their name consistently throughout the call.

3. Avoid the "umm" sound during conversation, don't get very excited and avoid saying things like "Yeah, this

	program ... " Also, don't use the word "great" too often.
Stage 4: Gap clarification The three levels of gap found	In this book, the gap clarification step focuses on helping the prospect paint a picture of their ideal future state at some point in the future by asking the right questions in the same way as in the previous phase. Sometimes I merge that phase with the exploration phase, since you will still be asking questions and uncovering where their desired future state lies, and what would be the ideal solution to their problems at a point in future, after 3, 4 or 5 years of months depending on the industry and the problems. The future state which they desire is also called the vision, and they can paint the vision for you if you ask the right questions. Remember they should paint the picture of the vision "future state" for you and this will only happen if you ask them the right questions. ***Note:*** *Do not ask question like these since they can harm your credibility as an expert. You should know the solution, not them. Also, in most cases, the prospects don't know the solution, and if they had known what to do, they wouldn't be on the phone with you in the first place.* **Avoid these questions at all costs:** 1. **What would be the best solution to your problem?** 2. **What would be the most "scalable, reliable, long-term, adaptive, agile or viable" solution which will take your business to the next level?** 3. **What would be the best way to align your current business process to the market demands?**

	4. **What adjustments do you think are necessary to target your ads to the right audience?** 5. **What type of refinement to your services will keep your services unmatched in this market segment after six months, one year or another time frame?** **Note:** You can form your own questions and practice them via roleplays. You don't need to memorize them. The main idea is to help you understand the way a closing conversation is carried out.
Stage 5: Prospect Gap-Selling Ask questions so that they sell themselves	In this step, your job is to do the groundwork by helping the prospect sell themselves on the gap. Meaning the prospects should tell you themselves during this step the reasons why they must act now. Once they sell themselves, this will mitigate objections since they themselves will tell you how urgent it is and how much it costs them. After this phase, the prospect has sold himself on the idea that filling the gap is essential. Therefore, this phase is called "prospect gap-selling." *"The future state which they desire is also called the vision."* **After revealing the desired future state, discover:** How urgent is it to reach that state? How much will it cost them? How important it is for their bottom line to get a solution and reach there? How much can it cost them during the time that passes monthly, quarterly, or yearly if they do not find a solution?

| Stage 6: Close "match features and desires."

Match the features to their vision

Close the prospect. | In this step, help them understand:

How your solution is going to help them in solving their problem

and

How your solution will provide them with the missing features, technology, mindset (in personal development B2C context), knowledge, frameworks and techniques etc., provided by you or your firm help them in going from the current state to their desired state.

Once that is done, you ask them whether they want to go ahead and take action or not!

Note: *Don't be pushy, don't become attached to the sale and only focus on solving their problem. This pattern interrupt will serve you very well. In other words, the more you sound, act and behave in contradiction with a stereotypical salesman, the better your chances of making a sale.* |

B2B examples using the blueprint script:

Now we describe the way a "generic script" can be applied in B2B contexts, such as real estate, software design industry, services sector, consultation industry and virtually any other B2B sales closing conversations as elaborated in Table 9. Notice that the surface level pains can vary widely depending on the product or service. Also, the various surface-level pains can result in similar financial and personal/emotional pains, and vice versa. The answers to the questions asked for uncovering the financial and personal pains are not mentioned in Table 9 for conciseness.

Surface level pains	Financial Pains	Personal/Emotional pains
Uncover Surface level pains them by asking questions like:	**Uncover Financial pains by asking questions like:**	**Uncover Personal pains them by asking questions like:**
What motivated you to be on call with me today?	How much did it cost them over the past 3/4/6 months or a year?	How has it impacted you emotionally?
How can I help you today?	Since the problem started, how much did it impact your bottom line?	How does that make you feel?
What is the biggest challenge you are facing in your business?	How many clients have you lost and what was the expected revenue per client?	How has it impacted your life as an entrepreneur/professional?
Potential answers to the questions depending on the current state:		How has it affected your well-being?
The Facebook ads are just not converting		How has it impacted your relationship with your family members and friends?
Our lead generation is not working, and our funnels need to target the right audience		
Our sales team is not closing enough calls each month.		
My supply chain software does not track things properly.		
My workforce is incapable of designing the software solution the client needs.		
The sales and marketing teams are just not communicating well.		
The PR campaign of competitors is way better than ours.		
Three of our clients have switched to the		

competitor in the past two months.		
Our business processes are highly inefficient		
The design methodologies we used for our software products are outdated. We need to train our software engineers with lean methodologies.		

B2C examples using the blueprint script:

The same generic script can be easily used in any B2C context, as elaborated in Table 10. Notice that the surface level pains can vary widely depending on the current state of the prospect. Different surface level pains can result in similar personal/emotional and financial pains and vice versa. Also, notice that the lower two levels of pains and the questions asked to uncover them are very similar to the B2B context. The answers to the questions asked for discovering the financial and personal pains are not mentioned in Table 10 for conciseness.

TABLE 10: APPLYING THE BLUEPRINT IN B2C CONTEXT.

Surface level pains	Financial pains	Personal/Emotional pains.
Uncover them by asking the right questions like: What motivated you to be on call with me today? How can I help you today? What is the biggest challenge you are facing in your life?	Uncover them by asking the right questions like: How much did it cost them over the past 3/4/6 months or a year? Since the problem started, how much did	Uncover them by asking the right questions like: How has it impacted you emotionally? How does that make you feel? How has it impacted your life as an entrepreneur/professional?

	it impact your bottom line? How many clients have you lost and what was the expected revenue per client?	How has it affected your well-being? How has it impacted your relationship with your family members and friends?
Potential answers to the questions depending on the current state: I am going through a divorce I don't have a work-life balance I cannot give time to my family My work has affected my health I don't have the right peer group to help me overcome my business challenges. My sleep patterns are crazy, and I never wake up refreshed. I don't get any fulfilment from my work. I cannot manage my finances well. One-third of my savings were lost due to one significant investment which failed miserably. I want to consult someone so that I don't make such mistakes again. How can I overcome the problem of not having fulfilling relationships?		

CHAPTER 27

Blueprint: How to Find Work?

After describing the generic script which will help you increase your closing rate in any industry, we now provide the blueprint which will help you land your dream closing job or clients in the industry which you love. The blueprint comes in the form of 16 points. If followed, it will put the odds in your favour no matter what your current situation is and no matter what your skill level is.

1. What are the different market segments in that industry?

2. How do the main competitors look in terms of market share, product or service features and core competencies?

3. What are the main problems in that industry?

4. What are the primary wants and desires of consumers or businesses served?

5. How is your partner, company, or person (doctor, influencer or authority in the field) positioned in the market?

6. What are the price points of the products or services offered by the competitors or experts in that industry?

7. If it is a service that you will sell, it is better to be a client first.

8. Get the feel of it. "Become a fan" of people or firms for whom you want to close. Go to events where their brand gets exposure. Check the social media channels where

they are active and try to meet people from the firm where you want to work in events.

9. Get business cards. Present yourself in the event as a problem solver. Be friends with the right people. Seek mentorship from the right people. Add key people in that industry to your social media accounts. Write articles on social media and share with the key people in that industry. Also, try to add renowned experts in that industry as friends on LinkedIn and other social media.

10. Keep on refining the CV as per your company's or influencer's needs and keep learning on Udemy and other online platforms about that industry to stay up to date.

11. Keep refining your LinkedIn profile and your Facebook profile so that it radiates the personality of a closer.

12. Make a motivation letter which reflects points 4 to 8 so that they can see the value that you brought them over social media. Isn't one hour a day of commenting and engaging on social media a good investment into your future? Compare that with four years in University for getting a bachelor's degree.

13. Apply for a job or send a private message on Facebook once you have given them value for 2-6 months. You can do that for several influencers, experts and companies in parallel.

14. The point is that you can think of these months as consolidation of your knowledge base for the industry so that when you start, you already have a sea of knowledge in your arsenal. That knowledge will give you an unfair advantage over others.

15. Post your success on Facebook groups and other online communities so that you can get noticed by influencers as well as entrepreneurs who can later contact you. If you have not yet landed a closing job or business partnership,

post videos and posts about your journey and what you think about different aspects of sales closing.

16. Learn, learn and learn when you have landed your dream job or business partners. There is always room for improvement.

CHAPTER 28

Blueprint: How to Become a top-notch closer?

Until and unless you continuously improve, develop the right habits and continually strive for excellence, you won't become the closer the market craves. Here are the 12 points which can be executed in any order to become one of the best closers in your industry. You can copy these points, create a checklist and start acting on these guidelines straight away.

1. Join the Facebook groups of closing communities.

2. Add closers to your social media and agree on roleplay times. Do as many roleplays as possible when you are not taking calls.

3. Only do roleplays with closers who have been in the industry for at least two years and have achieved excellent results. This is important because the only way to grow is to stretch your comfort zone. Ask them:

    i.   How well they close?
    ii. Any steps they follow?
    iii. Which call recording software they use?
    iv. How they track their results?
    v.   See which equipment they use for taking calls?

4. Discuss your recorded calls with the top-notch closers. If you have to pay for their time, do it. Remember, you will make 200-1000 USD+ on a single closing call, so why not invest 200 USD per month on this? You can earn ten times your money the next month, and you can record the roleplays so that you can listen to their

tonality and observe their closing style as many times as you like.

5. Work on your tonality during roleplays and observe how the other closer uses this potent weapon.

6. Make your own blueprint based on the words that you usually use and remember that nothing is set in stone. You can learn what works and what doesn't and keep modifying your script with time.

7. Do not memorize the script, but look at what each section or question in the script does. It is about the flow, tonality and control, and not about sounding like a radio station or robot.

8. Learn more about building rapport and objection handling. You will understand that many times, your lack of conviction, lack of detachment, mindset, shiny object syndrome, tonality, and inability to understand the problems of prospects causes objections. So, work on these areas. That is why this is not a book with merely a sales script or sales techniques. You have to work on the inside to create the world you desire on the outside. Your beliefs, your conviction, your certainty and your intent will project. You cannot escape them. So, work on them and change them to convert them into your most potent weapons.

9. Develop a routine. Without commitment, you are not going to reach your destination, as I always say!

Your future prospects are a consequence of your commitment and every commitment has a formal structure.

—Subayal

10. Be resourceful: If you don't have money for professional recording software, go with a free one in the beginning. If you cannot afford the course of an influencer for whom you want to close, team up with a friend and tell the influencer that you both want to take it. Most likely, he will love it. If you have kids or you are changing careers, remember that you can still learn the skills, and in fact you can learn anything. Just read my story; it is mentioned in the book for a purpose. If a guy from a third world country can achieve this much, can't you do a bit better or at least as well as I have done?

11. Develop a good work ethic which will become exemplary. Instead of watching TV for 2-3 hours, get on the phone, do roleplays, and you will see that after 1-2 months you will show noticeable improvement in your closing skills. Opportunities will only come if you are committed to a profession. Without taking action, nothing is going to happen for sure. Don't you think that by following these golden rules you will have a slightly better chance at improving your skill? Don't you know that if you don't take action, you will guarantee a bad financial future and average closing skills?

12. Take care of your health and dress for success, get regular exercise and get plenty of fresh air. Remember that when you take care of yourself, your wellbeing improves, and this improves your performance. When you dress well, you will feel better, and this will radiate in your voice. You will take notes, be more attentive, and focus better, all of which will drastically increase your closing rate.

CHAPTER 29

Blueprint: How to Master the Art?

In this chapter, we elaborate on the techniques for continually improving your closing skills. Roleplays are very important for continually learning and growing. With time, you will see a considerable improvement in your tonality, and you will also start to feel the impact of your tonality and questions on the other person. After every roleplay, always ask for feedback.

The feedback must cover the following areas.

1. **Identify the weakest area of your sales conversation.**

2. **Did you miss writing down any pain point?**

3. **Did you identify the personality of the prospect well?**

4. **What were your strongest points in the roleplay?**

5. **What were your weakest points in the roleplay?**

If you get very good at one of the aforementioned areas, switch to the other ones until you get good at all of them. We have listed these points in Table 11, which you can print and use for adequately tracking your sales conversations and roleplays.

TABLE 11: HOW TO TRACK YOUR SALES CLOSING PERFORMANCE AND IMPROVEMENT.

Identify the weakest area of your sales conversation.	Did you miss writing any pain point?	Did you identify the personality of the	What were your strongest points in	What were your weakest points in

		prospect well?	the roleplay?	the roleplay?
Uncovering three levels of Pains.	Pain point 1 Pain point 2 .			
Ability to dig into the level-3 pains.	. .			
Tonality.	. Last Pain point			
Making the prospect Painting the picture of future vision.				
Closing.				

Please remember that if you don't track your results, you will not know the areas in which you should improve in order to enhance your skill continually. Therefore, you should take into consideration the following lesson, which I learned the hard way.

Remember that the more you track your results, the more you will improve your skill, which will further fuel your passion for excelling and improving further.

—Subayal

At the end of each month, see how much you have improved in a specific area and how much more you should improve in order to make a positive impact on your results. At the end of the day, results matter, and the more you progress, the better the results.

I now present the concept of confidence and competence loops, which I devised in order to make sure that I master any skill I am learning or achieve any objective. This is done by continually measuring and tracking my performance. As you can see, in the confidence and competence loop, the main factors which motivate you to iterate over the loop constantly are the four Cs, which are *consistency, clarity, commitment* and *conviction*. That is why the first three sections of the book are so important. They build the mindset and explain the importance of working on your mindset and choosing the right identity. The right mindset and identity strengthen the four Cs and give you the focus and motivation to iterate over the loop over and over again until you have mastered the skill or achieved your objective. The confidence and competence loop is shown in Figure 11 and can be applied to learn any skill or accomplish any goal.

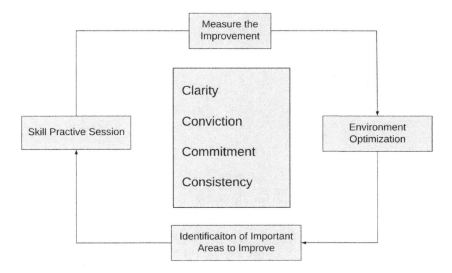

FIGURE 11: THE CONFIDENCE AND COMPETENCE LOOP THAT CAN BE APPLIED TO LEARN ANY SKILL OR ACHIEVE ANY OBJECTIVE.

We now elaborate on the way a confidence and competence loop can be used to master the closing skill and land your dream job or a client in the industry of your choice. You can see that the main drivers are the same, meaning the four Cs but the constant actions required to master a particular skill (in this case sales closing) are different as well as the way improvement is tracked or measured as you master sales closing. This is shown in Figure 12.

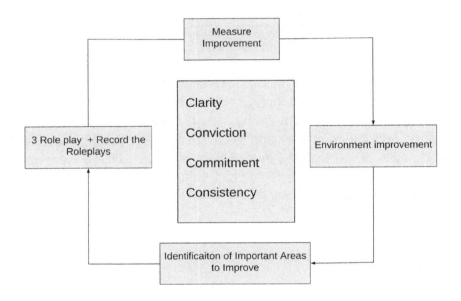

FIGURE 12: HOW A COMPETENCE AND CONFIDENCE LOOP CAN BE APPLIED TO MASTER THE SKILL OF CLOSING.

A confidence and competence loop can also be used to achieve a particular objective, such as landing your dream job or getting clients in the industry of your choice. You can see that the main drivers are the same, meaning the four Cs, but the constant actions required to achieve this objective are different as well as the way improvement is tracked. This is shown in Figure 13.

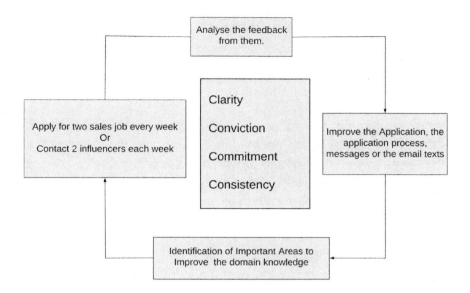

FIGURE 13: THE WAY A CONFIDENCE AND COMPETENCE LOOP CAN BE
USED TO LAND YOUR DREAM JOB OR CLIENTS.

CHAPTER 30

Blueprint: Building a team

E ven though the focus of this book is not recruitment or leadership, I firmly believe that these are the most critical areas when it comes to growth in a specific industry. As you grow in your career, you will get more recognition for your work, and one day you will be required to lead a team of sale closers for your clients. To form a power team, first of all, consider the closers with whom you have done roleplays or with whom you have taken some training so that you are sure that they are good sale closers. In all these cases, you must look at the following:

1. **Look at their previous work experience. Call the influencers or businesses where they worked before and ask for feedback.**

2. **How well do they understand the current state of the customers and how do they get them emotionally involved?**

3. **How was the closing rate of the closer, and do they have any video reviews from the influencers?**

4. **Tell them to send you a video in which they mention the reasons why they think that they will be a good fit for the team. Also, ask them about their closing experience. How will they add value to the team? You can see in the video how well they present themselves, their tonality, and also their overall personality.**

5. **Tell them to send you the recordings of their roleplays. Pay particular attention to:**

   i. **Their tonality and the way they uncover the level 3 pains. Without revealing the pains, they won't be able to achieve a good closing ratio.**

ii. How well they help the prospects paint a picture of their future state. That will uncover the gap which they want to overcome.

iii. How well they help the prospects cost the problem themselves.

iv. Are they listening most of the time or talking most of the time?

v. Do they sound like typical salespeople?

6. Do they have any certifications on closing?

7. Do they have sufficient time to close the leads provided to them properly?

8. Know the industry where they closed, for example, personal development, fitness, etc.

9. Do a roleplay with them yourself; after all, you will be working with them for a long time if they are selected, and this is the best way to gauge their skill.

10. See if they are coachable.

11. Evaluate their skills during the first two months, which can act as the test period. Give them one or two leads each day to test their skills.

12. Listen to the call recordings and evaluate the closing ratio.

13. See how well they qualify the clients. The last thing which you want is to enrol a person in a course where there are executives, and a person with unrealistic expectations or attitude problems joins it. It will be awful for the reputation of the course and your influencer.

14. The closer should be in a similar time zone as the countries from where most leads are coming.

15. Is the person a team player?

16. See from call recordings as to how well they help the prospect in selling the gap themselves.

17. Identify their personality type and see if they are a good fit for the team.

18. You must look for the following qualities among the candidates:

    i.   Creativity
    ii.   Hobbies
    iii.   Willingness to go the extra mile
    iv.   Domain knowledge of the business
    v.   Emotional intelligence
    vi.   Coachability
    vii.   Critical thinking

CHAPTER 31

Blueprint: Leading a Team

L eading a team is very important, since it will help you gain more visibility and get more clients. Good leaders nurture trust and conviction in the team via fair treatment of team members and via their emotional intelligence. They can pinpoint the areas where improvements are required; for example, in the IT processes or professional training for the team members. You can make use of technology to make things more streamlined and convenient to track. Here are the key points which you must take into account to effectively lead a team of sale closers.

Nurturing Skills and Helping Them Grow

1. The leads have to be equitably allocated, and if someone underperforms for a month or two, don't discourage them; try to provide support, training and mentorship. That person might be your best closer after six months. Therefore, the fair allocation of leads without favouritism is the best way forward to make people feel safe and secure.

2. Shuffle people around in different services or different products and see how well they do in various programs as far as closing ratio is concerned. Remember that you need to be careful there. You should avoid assigning a single service or product to one person on the team. Mainly where the price point is way too high, and others are earmarked for programs where the price points are lower. The financial incentive might deteriorate for the other closers, and it might lower the motivation an extra mile.

3. Allow them to grow, and meet them physically once in 4 months or a year depending on where they live.

4. A weekly meeting among the team members is a must, and you should inform them of the way marketing is done. They should have a line of sight of the way funnels videos are and what the customer has watched before coming to the call. Make sure that watch the webinars or ads which customer has seen so that they can incorporate this information in their closing calls. They should at least know if the customers already have the information about the value proposition of the product or service.

Using Software Technologies

Always use a program such as schedule-once which will automate user data collection from the forms in the sales funnels and route that data to a CRM. In this way, the closers can get an idea of the current state before the current call and what the product or service can do for them. That will help the closers brainstorm questions before the call to uncover the pains and drill down to the level 3 pains.

1. The customer books a call instead of the closer. That pattern interrupt is vital, since this positions the closers as breakthrough specialists, transformation specialists or product experts. Now, they are not the stereotypical salespersons which the parents don't want their kids to become.   That in itself will significantly increase the closing ratio.

2. Discipline is necessary for your success. Always develop email templates which the closers can easily modify to save time. Remember that in this way, you will also be able to see what works and what doesn't work in the long run. Remember that if you cannot measure it, you cannot improve it.

3. Use a CRM such as close.io, which will provide all the essential information and functionalities in one place. Meaning, the closers can call from within close.io, and

they can see the data of the form which the customers filled before booking the call. They are also able to record the calls, change the status of the leads, and also send voice messages from within CRM. That will keep things open and easy to track. Even if your CRM is not an almost all-in-one solution like close.io, you must use one which has all the essential features, is more intuitive, and is more reliable.

4. Track the status of the leads and automate the generation of the reports for easy tracking of the results from different perspectives so that you can maintain a healthy pipeline.

If you take into account the points mentioned above, they will set you up for success as a leader in the sales closing industry.

CONCLUSIONS

Here are the key findings which can be drawn from the concepts, techniques and techniques covered in this book. It is imperative to understand that these five points are a condensed form of the knowledge which I gained the hard way, after several failures and stressful days.

1. Sales closing is a skill which anyone can master and use to earn good money.

2. As far as the skills are concerned, the body language and tonality are the most critical parts of a closing conversation, and they will improve with time. After a few months of role-plays and closing calls, you will feel that you can connect more easily with prospects. Also, you will also be able to uncover the level three pains most of the times.

3. Your mindset and identity are the essential foundations for your success in your closing career. Without them, you cannot build a successful closing career. Choose your identity wisely and work on your mindset; it will transform you into a top-notch closer much faster.

4. Do regular roleplays and identify the areas of improvement. Once you do that, you can focus on these areas in your future roleplay sessions. In this way, your weaknesses will transform into your strengths at a much faster pace.

5. When you grow in your closing career and get opportunities to lead teams, you must ensure the fairness in lead allocation and nurturing the skills of the team members. You should make full use of technology to track the results to identify areas of improvement. These will set you up for success and exponential growth.

Dr Subayal Khan offers "The Nonconformist Salesperson" Sales training for B2B and B2C organizations of all sizes. To learn more or for booking a Sales training, visit us at: www.subayal.net

THE **NONCONFORMIST** SALESPERSON® *TRAINING*

ABOUT THE AUTHOR

Dr Subayal Khan is the Director and CEO of Subayal Consulting Limited. He has decades of B2B and B2C sales experience. He has trained many salespersons and entrepreneurs over the last two decades. Dr Subayal Khan has influenced the sales training industry with his proved methodologies and techniques which have helped several organizations in considerably increasing their sales revenue. His understanding of human psychology and concreted research background has helped him in diagnosing the symptoms of problems which many salespersons and entrepreneurs face. Most of his teachings contradict with the way stereotypical salespersons approach sales. His emphasis on problem solving and understanding the challenges of the prospects is what makes his trainings so effective.

The innate desire and ability of Dr Subayal to solve intricate problems across multiple industries has given him the reputation and unique positioning in industry. Apart from his expertise in sales, he is a renowned business strategist and business mentor who has been the mastermind behind several disruptive innovations and blue oceans. His intellect has won him several awards and distinctions from European Union and renowned research institutes and Universities.

In my free time, I enjoy great discussions with Mr Pa Joof and Essa Joof on different topics where my crazy unconventional views on society, human psychology and business act as a good source of entertainment. Also, I like downhill skiing, reading books and spending time in Finnish nature.

CONNECT

Websites: www.subayal.net

https://www.linkedin.com/in/subayalkhan/

https://twitter.com/subayalaftab

https://www.facebook.com/khansubayal/

REFERENCES

(Viktor E. Frankl, 1946)

Man's Search for Meaning: An Introduction to Logotherapy" by Viktor E. Frankl.

Paperback: 189 pages

Publisher: Simon & Schuster; 3rd edition (1 Jan. 1986)

Language: English

ISBN-10: 0671244221

ISBN-13: 978-0671244224

(Tony Robbins, 2019)
https://www.tonyrobbins.com/, accessed on 12th December 2019

(Karlskrona, 2019)
http://www.visitkarlskrona.se/en

(Les Brown, 2019)
https://lesbrown.com/about/

(Bob Proctor, 2019)
https://everipedia.org/wiki/lang_en/bob-proctor

(TU WIEN,2019)
https://www.tuwien.at/en/

(Neurolinguistic Programming, 2019)
https://neurolinguisticprogramming.com/, accessed on 12th December 2019.

(Aldo Civico, 2019)
https://www.aldocivico.com/

(Carl W. Buehner, 2019)
https://en.wikipedia.org/wiki/Carl_W._Buehner

(Bicester Village, 2019)
https://www.tbvsc.com/bicester-village/en

(Investopedia, 2019)
https://www.investopedia.com/terms/h/hindsight-bias.asp

Printed in Great Britain
by Amazon

60102773R00119